# BEYOND the BOMB

## LIVING WITHOUT NUCLEAR WEAPONS

*A Field Guide
to Alternative Strategies for
Building a Stable Peace*

**Mark Sommer**
*for the Exploratory Project on the Conditions of Peace*

FOREWORD BY
**KENNETH E. BOULDING**

DRAWINGS BY
**ED KOREN**

EXPRO PRESS

**Permissions to Reprint**

Israel Charny, *How Can We Commit the Unthinkable?* Copyright © 1982 Westview Press, Boulder, Colorado.

*Defence in the Nuclear Age* (1959) published by Fellowship Publications of the Fellowship of Reconciliation, Box 271, Nyack, NY 10960.

Daniel Deudney, *Whole Earth Security* (1983), Worldwatch Institute.

Richard Falk, "Contending Approaches to World Order," *Peace and World Order Studies: A Curriculum Guide* (Third Edition), World Policy Institute, 777 UN Plaza, NY, NY 10017.

Dietrich Fischer, *Preventing War in the Nuclear Age* (Totowa, NJ: Rowman & Allanheld, 1984), pp. 108, 113.

Randall Forsberg, "Confining the Military to Defense," *World Policy Journal* (1984), 777 UN Plaza, NY, NY 10017.

Robert Johansen, *Toward an Alternative Security System,* World Policy Institute, 777 UN Plaza, NY, NY 10017.

George F. Kennan, *The Nuclear Delusion: Soviet-American Relations in the Atomic Age,* © Pantheon Books, a division of Random House, Inc.

Joel Kovel, *Against the State of Nuclear Terror* (1984), published by South End Press, 116 St. Botolph Street, Boston, Ma. 02115.

Earl Ravenal, *Defining Defense: The 1985 Military Budget,* published by the Cato Institute, 224 Second Street SE, Washington, D.C. 20003.

*Voter Options on Nuclear Arms Policy,* published by the Public Agenda Foundation (1984), 91 pages. The complete study is available from the Public Agenda Foundation, 6 East 39th St., NY, NY 10016.

Alan Wolfe, "Nuclear Fundamentalism Reborn," *World Policy Journal* (1984), 777 UN Plaza, NY, NY 10017.

Published by Expro Press, Massachusetts
Distributed by The Talman Company
150 Fifth Avenue, New York, N.Y. 10011

© 1985 by Mark Sommer
First printing

Library of Congress Cataloging in Publication Data
Sommer, Mark
    Beyond the Bomb
    Includes index
ISBN 0-936391-00-6

Cover and book design by Laurel Marx

# FOREWORD

A useful metaphor for the present condition of the human race is that we are all living on a large tableland surrounded by cliffs of different sizes, what in the West is called a "mesa." The tableland has parts that are much more pleasant than others, but on the whole we can wander over it without coming to much harm. The cliffs, however, are another matter. Some are not too high or steep. If we go over them, some of us, at any rate, crawl back up again. Some cliffs, however, are a mile high and sheer. If we go over them we never come back. The tableland is peace. The cliffs are war. The high cliffs are nuclear war, from which there may be no return. We dash about on this tableland rather blindly. It is not surprising that sometimes we fall over the cliffs, especially if we gallop towards them. Sometimes we go to the cliff, as we did in the Cuban crisis under Kennedy and we draw back. Sometimes we start down what seems like an easy slope at the edge of the tableland, as in Vietnam—

but it gets steeper and our momentum gets greater. We lose a great many lives before we draw back.

It is clear that falling over cliffs is a poor method of learning about them. Falling over a mile-high cliff is no method of learning about it at all. We are all dead. What this book is about is how we learn about these cliffs without falling over them, how we learn to draw back when we approach them. In the last fifty years there has developed a small group of scholars and thinkers, some of whom think of themselves as peace researchers—some of them might not claim that title—but all of whom are concerned with finding out about cliffs without falling over them, studying the geography of this mesa and the way in which the human race charges around it, with a view to putting in warning signals where the cliffs are, especially those that are hard to see when we are dashing about on the tableland. This takes specialized knowledge. The ordinary experience of daily life, and even political life, is not enough. The cliffs change all the time. There are earthquakes—like the invention of firearms or the development of the nuclear weapon and the guided missile—which create cliffs where none existed before. Then it is very hard to know where they are. To use another metaphor, there are regions of time as well as regions of space, at the boundaries of which the basic constants and conditions of the system change.

When we go from one region of space to another, as when to go from the land into the sea, we are all aware that the system changes profoundly. What we know about living on the land does not prepare us at all for living in the sea. Similarly, when we go from one region of time into another, the experience of the past region is a very poor guide to the future. One of the great dangers in the world today arises from the fact that most people in positions of power learned a lot of what they think they know about the world in the period around the Second World War. Now, however, the world is very different from what it was like, shall we say, in the 1930s. Those whose image of the world was formed in the 1930s or thereabouts are often living in a very unreal world and do not know where the new cliffs are.

This succinct and well written little volume could almost be described as a guide to the new cliffs. It is an excellent account of an important part of the body of research and the thinking which have grown up in the twentieth century, especially in the social sciences, around the problem of conflict and its management. Something like a new discipline has developed in the social sciences, especially in the last fifty years, which studies the pattern and dynamics of conflict in society and how society is organized by conflict, just as economics studies how society is organized by exchange. The French have a name for this, *polemologie,* but this seems to be too much of a mouthful in English, and it is perhaps better to call it "conflict studies" with an applied field in conflict management. It has applications to many areas of human life—to personal, domestic, religious, organizational, and political conflict.

The most urgent application is certainly in the field of international conflict and war and peace. This volume summarizes with great skill an important part of the work in this area. It is not intended to be complete, like an encyclopedia, but it will give every reader a guide to the thinking and research that have gone into this field and which constitute one of the greatest hopes for human survival. Mark Sommer and the Exploratory Project on the Conditions of Peace have increased the chance of human survival by producing this volume. It should be widely read and pondered.

– **KENNETH E. BOULDING**
Institute of Behavioral Science
University of Colorado, Boulder

# ACKNOWLEDGMENTS

Most research borrows and learns from the work of others. In the case of this survey, the debt is especially large. I am appreciative of the generosity (and in some cases hospitality) extended by the many researchers in Europe and North America who shared their insights with me. Many find mention in this book but many others do not. Of my European colleagues, I would especially like to express my gratitude to Michael Randle and April Carter of the British Alternative Defence Commission, whose collegial example inspired those of us who founded Expro; Nigel Young of the University of Bradford and Colgate University, whose indefatigable efforts to create transnational networks among peace researchers and educators connected me with a great many I would not otherwise have met; and Adam Roberts of Oxford, whose clarity of thinking helped clarify my own. Others especially deserving of mention include Mogens Godballe, Hylke Tromp, Horst Afheldt, Jens Thoft, and Anders Boserup.

Among my colleagues in the United States, I would like to express my appreciation to all the members of Expro, for whom this report was originally written, and to the consortium of funders who underwrote the research. In particular, comments and encouragement from Dietrich Fischer, Robert Holt, Kermit Johnson, Helen Kelley, Bob Irwin and Kirkpatrick Sale proved especially helpful. Among other researchers whose thinking sparked my own are Kenneth Boulding, Freeman Dyson, Richard Falk, Roger Fisher, Harry Hollins, Robert Johansen, Gene Keyes, Saul Mendlovitz, Gene Sharp, Richard Smoke, and Bill Ury. Perhaps most of all, I owe a debt of gratitude to W.H. Ferry, whose persistence and perspicacity have contributed more than any other single factor to the founding of Expro and the publication of this book.

And finally, I wish to thank my wife, Sandi, who shared with me the trials of trekking student-class across Europe in search of new ideas, and who sustained me past all the inevitable doubts and discouragements to the long-sought completion of the project.

I take heart in the renaissance of positive thinking now emerging from the rubble of our shattered illusions and broken dreams. I offer this report in appreciation and celebration of its rebirth.

# TABLE OF CONTENTS

# INTRODUCTION

The Bomb has been with us now one full generation. For those of us who grew up with it, there is no living memory of a time when it did not exist. For those who grew up without it, the memory, still live and anguished, is of war—against which even a precarious cease-fire may seem preferable. In neither generation does there yet exist a belief in the possibility that we could ever shed our fascination with the Bomb. Though it is only one among a thousand generations that have carried us into this moment, we cannot yet imagine a time past the nuclear age.

Nearly two years ago I was asked by the founders of Expro to make "a preliminary survey of the territory beyond nuclear deterrence." At certain hard moments since that time, I have wondered mightily whether, given the contrary swell of current political tides, such a place could exist in any territory other than the imagination. I have gone looking for evidence of life beyond the Bomb in a dozen traditions of alternative thought that have accumulated in the years since its birth, reading as widely and deeply as time would allow. I have also made extensive pilgrimages in the United States and both Europes (West and East) to speak with theorists of social and political change.

Nowhere have I found ready answers, but many places I've found hints, traces, evidence of possibility. Working largely in isolation from one another and without financial resources, thinkers and researchers have been seeking, ever since the birth of the Bomb at Trinity, to conceive ways to take us beyond it. Approaching the Beast from all directions, they appear at first (even to each other) to be describing different animals. And indeed, the literature they have produced is often disparate and unconnected, written for specialists in the field and unread even by those in neighboring disciplines.

There is as yet no integrated vision of a world beyond the Bomb. Even to assert that such a world is possible requires a great leap of imagination, a willed suspension of disbelief. What we have at the moment is a kaleidoscope of images evoked by highly independent and sometimes eccentric imaginations, which nonetheless bear a certain familial resemblance. Our task at this juncture is less to reconcile conflicting perspectives than to extend the insights we already share into a comprehensive alternative understanding of the problem and its possible solutions.

I suspect that no one working alone is capable of managing this gargantuan task of integration. I have not even attempted it here. Being less than expert in a number of the fields surveyed in this report, I have had to compress the learning process from what should have been years to mere days and weeks, a feat of intellectual gymnastics I hadn't had the pleasure of performing since college days. This report is a not a conclusive statement but a working paper, a shared resource for an open-ended inquiry still in the process of definition. It is intended more as a set of questions than a set of answers.

I have organized the survey into a dozen fields of study roughly congruent with established, albeit unorthodox, intellectual traditions. They are presented not in order of actual importance (by which they might well be reversed) but in order of apparent immediate relevance to the question at hand. Thus, matters of hardware and policy first (because we are inclined to think the problem is technical in nature), the software of changed habits and attitudes later. But the most interesting and illuminating questions remaining to us may be more of culture than of policy. Recognizing that even our most elegant and appropriate solutions remain irrelevant if there is no will to enact them, I have explored, in an epilogue, the nature of our non-rational attachments to the Bomb and the effects of its ever-growing presence upon us. Much of the material in this chapter is necessarily speculative, since attitudes and emotions are not readily quantified. I have ventured here a step beyond the reporter's assignment in order to ask what needs and fears bind us to the Bomb and what we might need to do to break out of that bondage.

Nearly all the fields surveyed in this report have emerged during the past twenty years. Some, like alternative defense and security, have not yet established themselves as fully legitimate disciplines. Several are such close cousins that it is sometimes difficult to make meaningful distinctions among them. Thought that is by its very nature interdisciplinary and integrative will not passively remain within the tidy boundaries of academic classification. Categories overlap and include one another. The labels are dispensable. The structure of this inquiry has been purely functional: in my own mind still lacking an integrated understanding of the problem and a fully coherent vision of its resolution, I must present you with the fistful of fragments I have found, hoping that together we may arrange them into something whole and true.

# ALTERNATIVE DEFENSE:
## Protection without Threat

*"Offense sells tickets. Defense wins games."*

– MOTTO OF PACIFIC NORTHWEST
BASKETBALL PLAYERS ASSOCIATION

Offense and defense have played out a curious cat-and-mouse relationship in the history of warfare. While the attack has always held sway in the human imagination, there have also been memorable episodes of heroic defense—the Battle of Britain, the Warsaw Ghetto uprising, the siege of Leningrad, to name only the most recent. In both technology and tactics, offense and defense have tracked one another in a desperate pursuit of elusive unilateral advantage, the offense probing for a hidden weakness, the defense seeking hidden strengths. In various eras and circumstances new weapons and new strategies have temporarily thrown the balance from one to the other. But at no time has the offense so overwhelmed the defense as since the advent of nuclear weapons.

Ironically, it is also nuclear weapons, those paramount instruments of offense, which have taught us both the insufficiency of defense and the absurdity of attack. Yet both superpowers have continued to act as if a more devastating offense were in fact the only defense.

> *As threats echo and escalate, we may find that we have not* de- terred *war but merely* deferred *it until the results are assured to be utterly cataclysmic.*

The term, defense, has thus been so muddled by misuse that most Americans—and probably Soviets as well—can no longer imagine a defense that does not rely almost solely upon apocalyptic threats. Yet one need not be a prophet to recognize that there is no long-term stability to be found in a system of mutually induced terror. As threats echo and escalate, we may find that we have not *deterred* war but merely *deferred* it until the results are assured to be utterly cataclysmic.

Recognizing the peril and futility of a system of ever-enlarging threats, a number of theorists, first in Western Europe and more recently in the United States, have begun to ask themselves whether and how a defense might be fashioned that does not depend on threats and yet does not diminish one's own security. The past several years have seen the emergence of a new body of theory lying somewhere between disarmament and arms control. Many of those who now design alternative military strategies have migrated from their first and more familiar homes in the nonviolent tradition. A number of the theorists who first explored the potentialities of civilian resistance have, a decade later, chosen to focus on more intermediate possibilities. In most cases the shift has been guided by pragmatic considerations: civilian resistance was thought to be a "better idea" but simply beyond reach, at least within the next generation, and then perhaps only in those few nations outside the strategic equation of the superpowers, among a highly evolved and homogeneous people.

## Principles of a Defense without Threats

In choosing to examine alternative forms of military defense, these researchers have mostly tried to apply the principles and spirit of nonviolence to the hardware and strategy of armed force. All are aware of the compromises this course entails, the extent to which nearly any use of existing military hardware is destructive and violent in nature. Granting this limited set of choices, they have sought to draw a distinction between offensive and defensive capabilities, between destructive and protective strategies. They are endeavoring to reclaim the original meaning of the term, defense, from the inverted definition it has been given by post-war nuclear strategists: defense not as the capacity to inflict attack but as the capacity to repel it. These new strategies for a defense without threats have gone by a variety of names—**defensive deterrence, defense without offense,** and **non-provocative defense,** to mention just a few—but the principles underlying them evince a remarkable similarity. They include:

1.    greatly reducing our reliance on nuclear weapons, both strategic and tactical;

2.    greatly increasing our reliance on weapons more useful for the defense than the offense, making ample use of recent advances in defensive weapons technologies like precision-guided munitions;

3.    developing tactical military strategies strong in the defensive mode and deliberately weak in the offensive, to signal adversaries that they need not fear attack, yet that they will not succeed if they themselves attack. A no-first-use declaration by NATO, accompanied by a shift from tactical nuclear weapons to short-range precision-guided munitions, is one such strategy that has been given much consideration;

4.    adding a variety of non-military and nonviolent forms of defense, from prepared civilian resistance to economic sanctions and incentives and diplomatic initiatives;

5.    confining the task of defense to the territory, people, and institutions of one's own country and eschewing most claims beyond one's borders.

# European Research

Most of this new thinking has emerged from Western Europe— from Scandinavia, the Netherlands, West Germany, and Great Britain—where it has been seen in part as a means of supplanting the continent's hazardous dependence on nuclear weapons to deter a putative Soviet attack. Mainstream Western strategists have also been considering decreasing their reliance on tactical nuclear weapons for the defense of Western Europe, most notably in the ESECS study, *Strengthening Conventional Deterrence in Europe*,[1] but the thrust of their strategy is quite different. Instead of the strictly defensive posture advocated by alternative defense theorists, NATO Commander Bernard Rogers and others propose "deep strike" strategies utilizing advanced conventional weaponry to interdict Warsaw Pact second echelon troops before they reach the front. The fact that precision-guided munitions play a role in this conventional offensive demonstrates the troublesome convertibility of weapons. Proposed as a technological centerpiece for most alternative defense strategies, the anti-tank weapon can in fact be employed in the service of the attack, if the will is there to do it. The capacity for offense has not yet been bred out of them.

The most comprehensive and ambitious effort to translate the principles of a non-threatening defense to the particularities of a single nation has been the work of the

British Alternative Defence Commission. An independent committee of defense and disarmament specialists,
with a smattering of churchmen, MP's, trade unionists
and others, the Commission spent two years examining
the question of how Britain could defend herself without
nuclear weapons—both her own and those of the United
States. Their conclusions, set forth in a volume entitled
*Defence without the Bomb*,[2] call for a blending of a territorial military defense and a "fallback" capacity for civilian resistance. The Commission is currently embarked
on a second two-year study of a foreign policy to match
its reformed defense posture.

## Labour Party Adoption

It is a measure of the success of the Commission and
other groups in seeding their ideas in the political mainstream that Britain's Labour Party recently adopted a
non-nuclear stance as its official defense policy. The plan,
drafted by a committee of both left- and right-wing members of the party, proposes that Britain scrap its Trident
submarine program, decommission its Polaris missile system, and remove American military bases from British
soil. While Britain would remain in NATO, it would "ask
the United States and NATO as a whole to hold negotiations with Britain about the latter's withdrawal from the
West's nuclear defense planning arrangements . . . The
wording of the policy document is uncompromising," re-

ports The Christian Science Monitor. "Membership of (sic) NATO does not require member states to have nuclear weapons of their own or have U.S. nuclear weapons on their territory, or to accede to a strategy based on nuclear weapons. (Neil) Kinnock [new leader of the Labour Party] has pledged himself to support a policy line that would give Britain a leading role in advocating establishment of a non-nuclear defense for NATO.... Already it is obvious that if Labour comes to power, a serious crisis on defense matters with the United States is probable."[3]

Frank Barnaby and Egbert Boeker have devised in general terms a strategy of non-nuclear defense for the entire NATO Alliance. They propose the use of advanced conventional defensive weaponry in place of nuclear weapons (PGM's, electronic sensors, remotely piloted vehicles, etc). Indeed, their faith in the efficacy of a technical defense exceeds that of many of their colleagues. They also propose a gradual phasing-in of an East-West treaty of non-provocative defense, with intermediate steps to proscribe first use of nuclear weapons and then to forbid them altogether. This suggestion bears a resemblance to proposals for "qualitative disarmament" first conceived between the two world wars. "European security is possible without nuclear weapons," Barnaby and Boeker conclude. "It is impossible with them."[4] Barnaby and several retired NATO officers have established an organization aptly titled, "Just Defence," to press for adoption by NATO of a non-provocative defense posture.

## American Thinking

The most comprehensive and detailed study to date of an alternative defense posture for the United States is the report of the Boston Study Group, a small colloquy of scientists and defense and disarmament specialists (including Randall Forsberg, author of the nuclear freeze's initial Call, and Philip Morrison, a physicist and participant in the Manhattan Project) which undertook a five-year examination of the American military budget and arsenal. First released in 1979 as *The Price of Defense* (and republished in 1982 as *Winding Down: The Price of Defense*), the report calculated that the United States could safely subtract forty percent from its defense budget without endangering its security. "The alternative military policy which we propose," the report states, "is not only safe, but actually safer than the present policy, even if there is no corresponding, constructive change in other countries."[5] The group specifies three categories it seeks to **reduce**:

1.  excess nuclear weapons in the American arsenal, including all weaponry useful for a first strike;
2.  most of the aircraft carriers, amphibious landing craft and lightly equipped land combat forces most useful for interventions in the Third World. Although it did not yet exist when the report was written, the Rapid Deployment Force established

under President Carter is just such a mobile invasion force;

3.    investment in the development of new offensive weaponry, both nuclear and conventional.

The forces the Study Group chooses to **retain** include:

1.    a small but invulnerable nuclear weapon force sufficient to retaliate but clearly inadequate to threaten a first strike;
2.    the heavily equipped land combat forces and tactical combat aircraft to be used in the defense of Western Europe;
3.    a largely unchanged force of surface ships and attack submarines, to protect the freedom of the seas.

More recently, Frank von Hippel and Hal Feiveson, both of Princeton, have initiated a study of the technical issues relevant to a negotiated regime of minimal deterrence. The Princeton study examines "an alternative future in which nuclear weapons play as little a role as possible in international politics and military planning. Nuclear weapons would still exist, but both superpowers would have adopted no-first-use policies and would retain in their nuclear arsenals only enough weapons to deter their use by other states."[6]

Neither of these studies advocates a defense without offense in quite the sense in which it is being proposed in Western Europe. Both continue to rely on a residual deterrent of mostly submarine-based nuclear weapons, and the Boston Study Group leaves in place a variety of existing alliance commitments. The difference between the approaches simply reflects the greater reach of current perceived American interests and power and the greater distance that must be traversed in order to reach a genuine defense without threats. American theorists are well aware of how much more difficult a proposition it is to conceive a United States without the Bomb than a Great Britain, for only Britain depends on the arsenal she has built (and then sits beneath the American umbrella for good measure), while entire alliances depend— or believe they depend—on the American nuclear arsenal.

## Live and Let Live

This emphasis on a defense-only military posture has recently been echoed in the proposals of three other well-known theorists. Randall Forsberg has conceived a mode of disarmament in which nations progressively shed the most offensively oriented components in their arsenals and strategies and leave intact only those elements useful for the defense of one's own territory.[7] Jonathan Schell, formulating what he calls a deliberate policy to abolish nuclear weapons, chooses to leave in place a conventional arsenal with a strictly defensive orientation.[8] And Freeman Dyson, wearing twin hats as both weapons designer and peacemaker, has urged in two widely read books published during the past several years[9] that the United States, and as many other nations as it can persuade to follow, adopt a "defense-dominated future." "A good military technology," he writes, "is one that leads away from weapons of mass destruction and toward weapons that allow people to defend their homeland against invasion without destroying it."[10] Terming his policy "live-and-let-live," Dyson argues that "the fundamental change in objective is that we look to a defense-dominated balance of non-nuclear forces rather than to an offense-dominated balance of nuclear terror as the ultimate basis of our security."[11]

Although he urges that the transformation be negotiated, Dyson also allows for the possibility of generating a spontaneous process of benign imitation:

Our technology, if we care to use it for this purpose, gives us a uniquely effective means for guiding Soviet policies in directions which we may consider desirable. This channel of communication has the advantage of being always open. Soviet leaders do not always wish to listen to our diplomacy, but they always listen to our technology. We cannot use technology to persuade them to move in directions which they consider contrary to their interests. But our technology can influence them effectively whenever, as often happens, we wish them to move in a direction where their interests run parallel to ours. The move to non-nuclear defense is a case in point. If our technologists lead strongly into non-nuclear defensive weaponry, it is a good bet that theirs will follow suit.[12]

---

## Transarmament, Nonmilitary Defense, and Dissuasion

---

Peace researcher Dietrich Fischer has gone farthest in conceiving a comprehensive general theory for a defense without threats. Drawing on the example of Switzerland's territorial defense, Fischer advocates **transarmament,**[13] which he defines as a shift from offensive armed force to defensive military and non-military strategies. He terms this shift a "robust solution . . . an approach to the prevention of war that works regardless of the actual intentions and capabilities of the opponent, whether he has aggressive aims or seeks cooperation, whether he acts independently from what we do or reacts to our policies, whether his offensive and/or defensive capabilities are strong or weak."[14]

Fischer is especially insightful in his analysis of non-military defense (not to be confused with civilian-based defense) and its relation to a defensive military posture. He suggests four strategies: **1.** increasing the losses of an opponent if he attacks (through a loss of trade, exchange, prestige, and other benefits he enjoys in peacetime); **2.**

reducing the gains of an opponent in case he attacks (publicizing in advance one's plans to demolish anything of tactical value to an invading army); 3. reducing the losses of an opponent in case he does not attack (refraining from hostile acts, reducing and/or eliminating threats); and 4. increasing the gains of an opponent in the event he does not attack (through exchanges and trade of all sorts). Taken together these policies constitute what Fischer calls **dissuasion,** "a form of non-threatening deterrence which, without evoking fear, aims at convincing an opponent that keeping peace is better for him than resorting to war."[15]

## Merits and Deficiencies of a Defensive Strategy

Taken together, these theories display a remarkable convergence of perspective in a research community that is not inclined toward consensus. The merits of a purely defensive strategy are clear. Posing no threat to adversaries, it thus eliminates any provocation or justification for attack. The relinquishment of threats evaporates at least half the fuel for the arms race between East and West. Further, a defensive strategy would greatly reduce reliance on nuclear weapons, which are by nature offensive systems; whether it could eliminate them entirely is an open question. A defensive strategy is ethically more satisfying than MAD in that it returns defense to its original meaning and function—protection instead of destruction. And finally, "defensiveness" does not ignore the possibilities of harm and the requirement of shelter in an often hazardous environment.

But defensiveness is not without its deficiencies, limitations that the theorists themselves may know most acutely. It is no doubt wiser to face these difficulties directly at the outset than to pretend to an infallibility that cannot be promised to any single strategy, any means of defense. Defensiveness taken by itself is an incomplete policy and concept, a reactive rather than a creative strategy. It is perceived as too passive, too apparently vulnerable a stance to attract the expansive energies of nations and peoples accustomed to taking leading roles in world events. We may deplore these assertive energies and the destructive means by which they often vent themselves but we can't wholly deny an outlet for the energies themselves. In addition, purely defensive strategies do not meet the challenge at its source but at its outcome, where the full force of the attack has been marshalled and concentrated, placing the defender at a distinct disadvantage, both psychological and strategic.

> *One must be tough-minded enough to anticipate an adversary who will push even when not shoved.*

Having stripped itself of all means to press the initiative, a purely defensive strategy appears to lay itself open to mischief.

In foreclosing use of offensive weapons and strategies, a purely defensive strategy may be placing itself at a critical disadvantage in relation to an adversary who does not forswear their use. The abandonment of threats, while a most welcome act in itself, will not wholly eliminate the possibility of threats from the other side. One must be tough-minded enough to anticipate an adversary who will push even when not shoved. This is not worst case thinking but simple prudence. So a defense without threats must be doubly or triply strong in its purely protective capability, for it must meet an adversary undistracted by the need to fend off the blows of another and fully concentrated on the attack. No defensive strategy can promise invulnerability, a recognition that has led even those military planners who seek no territorial claims beyond their own borders to argue the necessity of some means of carrying the battle back to their adversaries.

## Defense Seen as Threat

And finally, there is no simple distinction to be drawn between offensive and defensive weaponry. It might well be observed that one man's defense is another man's threat. The function of a weapon depends as much on how it is deployed as on what it can do. Thus even short-range aircraft become potentially offensive weapons when placed in close proximity to the borders of conflict. Yet they may be designed and deployed for use as interceptors. There is little in the plane itself that prevents its offensive use. Indeed, aircraft designs increasingly include both offensive and defensive functions in order to eliminate the costs of making two different planes. Thus we return to the gauzy realm of intentions, uncertain and incalculable, and to the question of capability versus will. If your adversary has the means to kill you, does it mean he wants to? Most significantly, there is the irony of deterrence itself, an overwhelming threat ostensibly used as a "defensive" measure.

> *The great majority of nuclear weapons systems clustered under the umbrella of deterrence are in fact instruments of coercion.*

The distinctions between offense and defense will never be as clean as we would wish them to be, but that is no excuse for not making the distinction at all. Though the gray region is large, so is the black. The great majority of nuclear weapons systems clustered under the umbrella of deterrence are in fact instruments of coercion masquerading as those of protection. So although the distinction is not absolute, it is fundamental.

These evident limitations of defensive strategies are not immutable. But to get past them we may have either to expand our notion of defense or enlarge our repertoire of defensive strategies—or more likely both. In rightly forswearing aggressive designs, we need not choose passivity instead. We may need to clarify in our own minds the difference between offensive and initiative. An offensive is an assault, an attack, an attempt to seize control, the capacity to penetrate and devastate an adversary on his home ground. We are correct in challenging the ethics and efficacy of threatening such devastation. But in accepting this self-restraint, we should not also deny ourselves the independence and freedom of action that are initiative. Indeed, without such initiative, creative and active rather than merely reactive and defensive, we will not likely succeed in defending ourselves. Military strategists are correct in stating that no defense can succeed without some means of carrying the battle back to the adversary. Where they may well be wrong is in assuming the form of that offense to be an attack, executed with armed force. One can as well, and perhaps far better, assert one's freedom of action and take back the initiative by non-military means.

## Defending Both Sides from Harm

The very concept of defense may itself have become obsolete. For the term tends to confine our consideration to only one side of the conflict, one dimension of the struggle. Defense as traditionally understood looks only to the safety of one's own—most often at the expense of one's adversaries. Defending oneself has traditionally been viewed as a kill-or-be-killed proposition in which all outcomes are either victory or defeat and only one can win. That understanding may have been appropriate enough, though fearfully destructive, in prior centuries. But the advent of nuclear weapons annuls victory. Thus we must either stretch our consideration of the defense of the realm to include our adversaries or move to a naturally more inclusive concept that considers the fate of each party to the conflict and seeks to preserve *all* from harm. We extend this concern to our adversaries not from sympathy but from self-interest. We know well enough that if we do not look to their safety, we will have none ourselves. We can no longer gain security at their expense.

---

*Mutually protective strategies thus replace bids for unilateral advantage. The defense of one* includes *the defense of the other.*

---

This is a subtle but significant step beyond defensive thinking and opens the possibility of developing strategies that transcend polarities instead of reinforcing them. It is also a step beyond relinquishing threats (a necessary and laudable move, but insufficient in itself) in that it does not simply block the illegitimate use of one's own armed forces but indicates an alternative direction for assertive and independent action. Mutually protective strategies thus replace bids for unilateral advantage. The defense of one *includes* the defense of the other. What in the pre-nuclear age was a moral imperative has in the nuclear age become a practical necessity.

Yet this Olympian perspective may lie above our present perch. We are still saddled with nationally-based defenses composed of weapons which by their very definition and design are intended to provide security to only one side. So we may need to engage in a simultaneous process of relinquishment and redesign, giving up offensive weapons while inventing mutually preservative instruments and strategies. And we may need to reclaim defense from its illegitimate offspring, intervention and intimidation, as a transitional phase in moving our minds from unilateral advantage to common security.

---

## A Common Defense against the Bomb

---

"To provide for the common defense." The phrase is familiar to most Americans from the Preamble to the U.S. Constitution. When the words were first written, the definition of "common" comprised thirteen colonies on the eastern edge of the American continent. As the American empire expanded, so did the definition of the term, "common." Yet there was always a frontier where the common defense ended and the common enemy approached. Even now, both the United States and the Soviet Union cling to the Bomb as their "common defense" against each other. Yet the self-evident truth of this era is that the one overwhelming threat both sides face is not each other but the shared peril of annihilation. It is in just this sense that the phrase, "to provide for the common defense," takes on its most inclusive meaning: not "me" against "you," but both against the Bomb.

It may be that for those still more attached to national than global perspectives, expanding the definition of "common" to *include* their adversaries may supply the essential bridge between an obsolescent nationalism and a developing globalism. The world order thinking of peace researchers during the past few decades has yet to filter into the mainstream of political discourse. From our imagined perch above the melee, we may readily devise a more workable plan for global security. But for the moment the actors are still national: nations still make history as global entities as yet do not. We must thus find ways and means of translating new understandings of common security into the existing (and insufficient) paradigm of unilateral defense in order to overcome lingering resistances to new historical truths. "Think globally, act nationally," we might say, amending Rene Dubos' brilliant advice, "Think globally, act locally." Not because national actors are the best for the job but because they are for the moment the only ones with the effective power to make change. And even then, it is the common peoples of these nations who will need to force reluctant governments into providing for the common interest.

Theorists of alternative defense strategies are mostly quite aware of the limitations of perspective and possibility inherent in defensive thinking. It is generally seen as a strictly transitional strategy, a halfway house on the way to disarmament, a means by which to wean ourselves from our dependence on nuclear weapons without resorting to still other forms of destructive capability. Taken by itself, it may indeed constitute a technical fix, unlikely to be adopted and if adopted, likely to be harnessed to offensive weaponry in a new and more perverse Faustian bargain. But if adopted as one step among several or many, and if reinforced by more affirmative nonmilitary policies, alternative defense strategies could yet contribute to the emergence of a far less hostile environment than we now endure.

# QUESTIONS:

1.  One man's defense is another man's threat. The offensive capability of a weapon depends as much on its location as on its range and firepower. To what extent would arsenals need to be refashioned to assure a thoroughly defensive capacity?

2.  There is no perfectly invulnerable defense. Does a voluntary self-limitation renouncing the offense place the defense at an unrecoverable disadvan-

tage? How can a defense without offense regain the strategic initiative?

3.　What are the most likely threats to be defended against? The familiar scenario of a blitzkrieg may be wholly outdated. Invasion may not be nearly so likely as remote-controlled destruction and nuclear blackmail, against which both conventional military defenses and civilian resistance are largely helpless. How can these very different kinds of threats be addressed without resorting to nuclear counter-threats?

4.　Can non-military civilian resistance be united with a defensive military strategy without negating the strengths of each? What forms might this union take?

5.　Some of the politicians and generals on whom a defensive strategy is being urged may not in fact desire just protection of their own territory. Offensive weapons provide them with the tempting capacity to extend their influence well beyond their own borders. Don't proposals for a defense without offense run contrary to their own immediate self-interest?

6.　How would the Soviet Union and Warsaw Pact nations likely respond to NATO's adoption of a purely defensive posture? In what ways could the West encourage (or, if necessary, pressure) the East to respond in kind? What if they did not? Could public support for a defense-only policy be maintained in the absence of reciprocation?

7.     Adoption of a defensive military arsenal in the absence of corresponding changes in foreign policy might well revert to an offensive stance over time. What political changes should accompany the transformation?

8.     Is there any danger that in advocating a defensive military strategy these theorists will become seduced by hardware and lose sight of the larger goal of disarmament? Is this another technical fix?

9.     It may work for Switzerland, Sweden, and Yugoslavia, but can it work for a superpower with far-ranging interests and "responsibilities"?

10.     What would prevent this strategy from degenerating into a new arms race in "defensive" weaponry, grafted onto an already uncontrollable competition in offensive arms?

# ALTERNATIVE SECURITY:
## Not by Arms Alone

The arcane occupation of missile-counting has so long dominated debate about the basis of security in the nuclear age that most professional strategists, and with them the lay public, remain captive to the notion that security is primarily a matter of more or fewer weapons. Despite their more sophisticated models of politics, even traditional arms control advocates often feel obliged by the obsessively missile-bound mindset of the public discussion to define their alternative strategies entirely in terms of changed hardware—as, for example, in the mildly reformed, "leaner, meaner" defense championed in recent years by Senator Gary Hart and a small group of Congressional neo-liberals. And indeed, as we have seen, even the more radical proposals of alternative defense strategists choose to restrict their attention to changes of weapons and tactics.

Weaponitis, the Boston Nuclear Study Group terms this fixation, arguing that by allowing the debate to be artificially narrowed to questions of hardware we neglect the many non-military factors that contribute to or detract from national and global security. A small number of political theorists has sought in recent years to expand the definition of security to include a broad spectrum of non-military strategies and initiatives which taken together help make the resort to armed force less likely in the first instance. By an integrated foreign policy of economic incentives, diplomatic initiatives, development assistance, participation in institutions of global governance, and the like, and by a domestic policy that emphasizes a robust but non-exploitive economy, an equitable distribution of wealth, and a vital cultural life, a well-conceived alternative security system creates an environment in which the problem of defense is no longer so overwhelming a preoccupation in international life. It is the systematic integration of these policies so that they reinforce one another which distinguishes the alternative security approach from the more random and piecemeal proposals of the arms control community and the exclusively hardware emphasis of alternative defense thinking.

> *We neglect the many non-military factors that contribute to or detract from national and global security.*

## Elements of a Global Security System

Designs for alternative security systems vary in intellectual structure but they share similar purposes and values. Some propose strategies tailored to specific countries, nationally sponsored initiatives designed to prompt other states to follow suit and thus encourage the development of a safer and more equitable global system. Others begin at the global level and emphasize the need for more effective transnational institutions of governance. Robert Johansen lists five principles in what he calls a **global security system** that would serve the needs of citizens as well as states:

1.  "It tries to prevent the desire for short-range advantages from dominating decisions at the expense of long-run interests."

2.  "(It) emphasizes the importance of providing greatly expanded positive incentives rather than relying largely on negative military threats. . . . We can prevent any potentially aggressive government from precipitating a war if we can assure that, in the eyes of its governing officials, the benefits of peace outweigh the anticipated benefits of war."

3.  "(It) emphasizes a positive image of peace which includes much more than war prevention. . . . (1) the right to peace and to freedom from the threat of genocide and ecocide; (2) the right to security

    of person against arbitrary arrest, torture, or ex-
ecution; (3) the right to traditional civil and political liberties; and (4) the right to fulfill all basic
needs essential to life."

4.     "It moves beyond the familiar, singular focus on
security for one nation-state. . . . With a concern
for the security of the whole nation and the whole
human race, rather than merely for parts of either,
a new attitude toward 'foreign' societies develops.
The distinction between 'our' government and
'their' government begins to fade. . . . All governments become 'my' government."

5.     "The most vital front line of defense becomes not
a new generation of nuclear weapons but a new
code of international conduct to restrict the use
of military power."[1]

Uniting alternative defense strategies like those proposed in the previous chapter with a variety of non-military sources of security and strength, Johan Galtung
identifies four elements in an effective alternative security system:

1.     Transarmament from an offensive to a defensive
military posture;

2.     A gradual decoupling from superpower alliances;

3.     Strengthening one's inner invulnerability
(through cultivation of a sound and self-reliant
economy, a healthy ecology, and an equitable and
stable social system); and

4.     Enhancing one's "usefulness" to would-be adversaries, by sponsoring mutually beneficial trade and

providing valued services.

Regarding invulnerability, Galtung draws an insightful analogy with the health of the individual human body:

> The medical parallel is obvious: this is the capacity of the human body to withstand any insults . . . so that they do not have any 'bite'. The healthy body adequately nourished, clad, protected from the hazards of nature . . . is one important precondition. Another is the capacity of the body itself to fight off any intruder through the defense mechanisms of the cells of the human body . . . And beyond that, should the other two fail, it is the capacity of the body to engage in a more lasting cure, to undertake its own repair work. Hence, what we are looking for would be the mechanisms by means of which the social body could do the same, all the time drawing on its own resources, not being dependent on an outside that might be partly or wholly hostile.[2]

Several dimensions of self-reliance contribute to the inner strength Galtung believes essential to a nation's security: economic self-sufficiency, especially in basic needs during times of crisis; ecological stability, preserving sources of food and shelter; political autonomy, preferably within a federal system; domestic social harmony, to avoid being weakened by internal conflicts; and cultural identity, to provide a clear sense of communal purpose and shared values.

## Harnessing Information Technologies for Peace

Approaching alternative security from the perspective of high technology in the space beyond the Earth's atmosphere, Daniel Deudney asserts that the thinking and planning of both mainstream and alternative strategists have yet to recognize the impact of what he calls the transparency revolution on the security of all nations. "Advances in information technology—sensors, communication and processing—have created a rudimentary planetary nervous system, fragments of a planetary cybernetic. . . . This transparency revolution means that the traditional struggle between offensive and defensive military force has been transformed into a competition between the visible and the hidden—between transparency and stealth. . . . Planetary-scale information systems bring the strategic competition between the superpowers to its least stable and most dangerous state. At the same time these systems make planetary-scale security possible for the first time in human history. Within the planetary war machine at its most advanced, unstable state may lie the embryo of a new security order."[3]

Deudney specifies four steps toward an alternative security system: "a new, more open information order, limits on weapons innovation, cooperative science and the pacification of the commons. . . . Although a new security system would require the regulation of the largest-scale systems of human creation, this could be done within a minimalist world order. A new security system need cover only those problems that are irreducibly planetary in scale. . . ."[4]

## Dispelling the "Weapons Paradigm"

The Boston Nuclear Study Group is a gathering of six sociologists from Boston College and Brandeis University engaged in critical research and writing on nuclear policy. They believe the narrow technical focus of the nuclear debate around weapons and the arms race must be shifted toward a fundamental critique of foreign policy and the internal social forces that promote militarism. Using perspectives drawn from the social sciences, they seek to demonstrate that the risk of nuclear war arises primarily from an interventionist foreign policy and sociocultural assumptions not normally linked to the nuclear problem. They are working on a book that challenges the "weapons paradigm" to which they feel both hawks and doves are captive, critiquing the assumption that either building or reducing nuclear weapons can significantly affect the risk of nuclear war. They argue instead that a fundamental shift in the direction of foreign policy, involving a repudiation of military intervention in the Third World and a new disposition to support democratic governments, is far more important in reducing the risk of nuclear war. They are working on a second book that explores the cultural, psychological and sociological dimensions of the nuclear problem and points to the far-reaching social transformation necessary to make genuine progress toward a world free of the threat of nuclear war.

## Strategic Disengagement

Not all theorists of alternative security envision and require such sweeping social and institutional changes. Earl Ravenal represents a school of thought uniquely his own in the otherwise generally congruent ensemble of alternative security systems currently being proposed. Once a Pentagon policy analyst, he now proposes a set of policies wholly contrary to the "power projection" interventionism that typifies present Pentagon thinking. Deeply skeptical of the prospects for establishing a "just" and stable world order (although not unsympathetic to its values), Ravenal predicts an increasingly anarchical political universe and counsels a policy of "strategic disengagement" to hedge against events that cannot be managed or controlled: "Others may be tempted to measure such an anarchical world, with its liabilities, against the abstract desirability of controlling events, steering them in favorable directions. But—somewhat like deterrence—attempts at control, if they fail, can yield both greater implication and greater harm for the nation that has made the attempt. Whereas, if we avoid involvement, there may be disorder in the world, but we are compensated by the fact that we are not implicated in it."[5]

Ravenal proposes a "new strategic paradigm" to govern U.S. policy in a world of "general unalignment":

Instead of deterrence and alliance, we would pursue war-avoidance and self-reliance. Our security would depend more on our abstention from regional conflicts and, in the strategic nuclear dimension, on what I would call 'finite essential deterrence'. . . . Our military program would be designed to defend the most restricted perimeter required to protect our core values. Those core values are our political integrity and the safety of our citizens and their domestic property. . . . Over time, we would accommodate the dissolution of defensive commitments, including NATO, that obligate us contingently to overseas intervention.[6]

Ravenal's thinking has sometimes been dismissed as isolationist, but he maintains that a "strict and consistent" policy of military non-intervention can be well-mated with "a concern for constructive contact with the world. . . . The face of the policy would be hopeful and constructive, selectively accommodating interdependence—stressing practical cooperation in specific areas, encouraging the universal observance of an international law of self-restraint, and joining in the mediation of disputes and some limited but noncommittal peacekeeping. But the residual level of the policy would be skeptical and defensive, hedging and insulating against disorder."[7]

## An Alternative Security Budget

The Security Project of the World Policy Institute proposes a set of alternative military, foreign, and economic policies designed to cut $470 billion from the $1.720 trillion five-year projected Defense Department budget (leaving in place a still whopping $1.250 trillion). Its First Report proposes adoption of a "stable, streamlined defense":

1.    a nuclear deterrent force designed for the sole purpose of deterring "nuclear attack." (6000 warheads based on 31 Poseidon and 6 Trident I submarines);

2.    the adoption of a non-threatening defense of Europe that would encourage detente between East and West, allow for the gradual withdrawal of American forces, and raise the threshold between peace and war;

3.    a program of non-intervention, political reconciliation, and economic development that would contain and reduce conflict in the Third World; and

4.    expanded support for the building of international institutions of common security for international peacekeeping, monitoring of arms, and the peaceful settlement of disputes.[8]

The report proposes a superpower "non-intervention

regime," spearheaded by an independent U.S. pledge "not to send its armed forces to any country where they are not now present, even if invited."[9] Finally, in the realm of economic security, the report recommends a "full-employment, better-thy-neighbor" policy emphasizing the transfer of resources from military to "productive" activities, and a program of "public investment in the physical infrastructure and human capital" of the United States, to be called "USA-Works."

These sources constitute fragmentary evidence of the emergence of a new body of thought, but it is too soon to say whether alternative security should be understood as a separate category from its close cousins, world order, alternative defense, arms control, and disarmament. Its focus is substantially broader than alternative defense and arms control but not so Olympian in perspective as world order studies often are. Alternative security thinking is an effort to shake the public mind free of its reflexive tendency to associate security solely with military hardware. By identifying and strengthening the very broadest range of non-military approaches to security, it seeks gradually to wean nations and peoples from their dependence on armed force, not by the direct approach of abolition but by the more indirect strategy of substitution. This perspective is founded on the premise that nations will not be persuaded to relinquish their weapons, nuclear or otherwise, until and unless a safer means of securing themselves can be found and made to work. The invention of alternative security systems is one effort to meet that need.

# WORLD ORDER:
## As if People Mattered

*"A map of the world that does not include Utopia is not even worth glancing at."*

– LEWIS MUMFORD

As traditionally understood and practiced, the study of international relations concerns itself with an ostensibly objective accounting of the distribution of power among nations and the most likely shifts in that balance. Though so-called "human values" do sometimes enter into the equation, they are generally considered to be inappropriate to the presumed amoral universe of global politics—at best irrelevant, at worst a dangerous distraction from the central task of gaining and maintaining power. Even when such values are given consideration, they are most often mentioned in the context of defending national ideals rather than individual rights. Nations remain the elemental citizens of the global community while the citizens within them remain effectively disenfranchised.

During the past two decades a small but growing number of scholars has sought to establish a conception of international politics both more global and more local, more humane and more balanced. From its inception world order thinking has been a very broad category— indeed, almost the broadest imaginable. Early on in the life of the discipline, Raymond Aron distinguished five different meanings for the term, **world order**:

Two of the meanings were purely descriptive:
order as an arrangement of reality, order as
the relations between the parts. Two were ana-
lytical— partly descriptive, partly normative:
order as the minimum conditions for existence,
order as the minimum conditions for coexistence. The fifth conception was purely normative: order as the conditions for the good life.[1]

It is the fifth definition, the "normative" or ethical approach to world order, which has prevailed in what

has since come to be known as world order studies—
what Richard Falk, a leading exponent of the approach,
calls a "system-transforming" emphasis. The World Order
Models Project, initiated in 1968, drew together researchers from Latin America, Africa, Japan, Europe, the Soviet
Union, India, North America and elsewhere to define a
set of common values "general enough," writes Falk, "to
command consensus and yet distinctive enough to establish an identity. . . ."

This transnational group of scholars, therefore,
is committed to the search for peace with eq-
uity, and seeks to evolve a globalist ideology
that draws on liberalism to check the abuse of
state power in the relations between governments and people, on socialism to depict a humane set of economic relationships based on
societal well-being, on ecological humanism to
reorient the relations between human activity
and nature, and on global modeling to put
complex interactions of societal processes at
various levels of organization into a dynamic,
disciplined framework.[2]

The group designated five "preferred values" it sought
to realize in its modelling: peace, social justice, economic
well-being, ecological balance, and participation in the
governing process.

# WOMP: Reinventing the World

The World Order Models Project was, in the words of its director, Saul Mendlovitz, "a crazy thing to do, really," in its audacious attempt to reinvent the world as if people mattered more than states, as if ethical values counted as much as material. In this sense, WOMP began with a frank bias in favor of humanistic values that is wholly at variance with the sought-for objectivity of social science and the frankly self-interested strategies of practical politics. Its normative basis, its value-laden emphasis, is both its strength and weakness: its strength in that the motives and judgments are unimpeachable in principle, its weakness in that the perfection of justice seems to find few counterparts in highly imperfect human history.

Among world order thinking's important contributions to the question before us is its recognition that the attainment of a peace worthy of the name requires attention to much more than the prevention of armed international conflict, considerable and essential as that task is. Gross injustice and exploitation, poverty and hunger, environmental plunder and degradation, and powerlessness constitute an entire second tier of "structural violence," to use the term first employed by Johan Galtung.[3] The interpenetration of these problems, their negative synergy, assures that any effort to make peace without concern for them will likely unravel or become a mockery of the term. WOMP established from the outset the salience of these threats to the health of human culture and gave them equal status with the threat of armed conflict.

> *This replacement of people for governments as the primary beneficiaries of a world order is a quite revolutionary shift of emphasis.*

World order research more generally has established the legitimacy of a perspective of "global humanism" centered in no specific culture but embracing all of them, to supplant (or at least to coexist alongside) the traditional state-centered view of reality. This replacement of people for governments as the primary beneficiaries of a world order is a quite revolutionary shift of emphasis. The relative dearth of institutions and actors to represent this global perspective, however, has tended to lend the speculations of world order theorists an abstract, sometimes almost mathematical quality. Preferences have so overwhelmed realities that the histories and proclivities of particular nations, their likely behavior in a given set of circumstances, have sometimes been neglected. Richard Falk warns that we must not be "geopolitically naive," and the point is well-taken. Recent research has gone far to remedy this problem. Robert Johansen, for example, introduces specific case studies of U.S. policy in each of four categories of world order "preferred" values and compares their professed and implicit goals with a global humanist approach.[4] This empiricism helps to root speculations about possible futures in the rocky but perhaps still fertile soil of present circumstances.

A further contribution of world order studies has been their integration of a host of related disciplines which have until recently had little to say to one another. Richard Falk identifies nine major fields of study within the scope of world order inquiry: politics, history, economics, psychology, biology, anthropology, religion and culture, ecology, and astrophysics(!)[5] This astonishing breadth of perspective distinguishes the normative world order approach from most other disciplines studying the problem of war and provides a significant precedent for further interdisciplinary and integrative research in the future. "What is left out of such an image," writes Falk in urging an "enriched inquiry," "is the integrating sensibility that gives coherence to insights drawn from a variety of sources. Without such an integrative effort, the extended inquiry will not lead anywhere. Whether anyone has the capacity to carry out such an ambitious program of study is also to be considered. Perhaps it will require decades of 'preparation' until a genius of integration can unfold a generally acceptable conception of world order studies."[6]

## Transition Strategies: The Third System

The design of plausible transition strategies has always been the Achilles' heel of world order research. Recognizing that states themselves are in some respects the least likely actors to adopt a world order perspective (other than that world order which would maintain or advance their own positions of influence), world order theorists have looked elsewhere for the changes to begin. Cognizant as well of the dependent status of the United Nations and other fledgling international institutions, they suggest that we place considerable emphasis on what Falk calls the "Third System ... the system of power represented by people acting individually or collectively through voluntary institutions and associations ... The Third System is the main bearer of new values, demands, visions. . . ."[7]

In order to strengthen their links with this Third System of non-institutional movements, a number of the participants in WOMP have initiated an "independent commission for the study and promotion of a just world peace" (Popular Movements and Global Transformation). The emphasis of this commission's work will be placed on identifying those transnational and non-governmental "agents of change" which could contribute significantly to the realization of a just world order and seeking to "state common principles for local action ... in which local movements may join in complementary and supportive ways to achieve a set of concrete political objectives over the next two decades."[8]

Stressing that the initiative for change may need to begin with non-governmental actors, world order theorists Gerald and Patricia Mische urge the establishment of multi-issue coalitions and networks among religious, educational, and professional groups. "World order actors can be subnational, national, regional, international, transnational or global. They may be individual persons or they may be movements, organizations, or institutions. . . . Much depends upon whether or not [they] *believe* that they can be shapers of history . . ."[9]

## QUESTIONS:

1.  World government, seen as a last, best hope of mankind in the years following the Second World War, now elicits profound skepticism in most quarters. Why has the idea so much fallen out of favor?

2.  Some world order studies have been characterized by a faith in rational behavior that both history and psychology would appear to undermine. To what extent are we capable of enacting a planned and preferred future? What precedents are there for such sweeping intentional transformations and how have they fared?

3.  In recent years world order specialists have spoken more of global governance than of world government. What are the differences of approach implicit in this shift?

4.    Can nuclear weapons successfully be uprooted from their central position in world politics without a significant transformation of the global political and economic order? If not, what kinds of broader transformation are minimally necessary?

5.    The system-transforming tradition of world order posits a set of preferred values to be realized in a variety of alternative worlds. But with the radical diversity of values evident in contemporary global politics, can we expect to gain consensus on those which are to be preferred? And if we can agree on the terms, can we agree on their definitions?

# DISARMAMENT:
## The Road Not Taken

Disarmament is surely the most direct route into the territory beyond the Bomb. But it is also the road least likely to be taken, at least in the first instance. Over the years since the First World War, a great deal of careful and reasonable thinking has gone into the invention of sensible regimes for both general and nuclear disarmament. There is no lack of good arrangements. What has been missing, of course, has been the will to enact them. For the actors being asked to engage in these agreements, there is a large near-term loss of power and influence and at the far end only a vaporous promise of greater security. One might even conclude that these plans are perhaps too reasonable for the unreasonable nature of the beast they are designed to serve. Nevertheless they represent useful vehicles to take us where we want to go, if we could once firmly resolve to go there.

## Legalist Approaches

A quarter century ago Grenville Clark and Louis Sohn proposed what remains the most comprehensive and detailed plan yet devised for universal disarmament (*World Peace through World Law*, 1958; revised, 1966). Their legalist approach stipulated a strengthening of the UN Charter, and particularly of the General Assembly, to enforce disarmament and to manage disputes through an intricate system of formal institutions. Under the authority of the General Assembly a world "peace force" would be created, possessing the sole remaining legal recourse to nuclear weapons, to enforce disarmament and to prevent the spread of conflict between nations. The prohibition of national armed forces of any variety is absolute: "We should face the fact that until there is *complete* disarmament of every nation without exception there can be no assurance of a genuine peace," they wrote.[1]

Their plan, admirably thorough and reasonable in its propositions, did not, however, attract the political support that would give it contemporary relevance, and over time its prospects have still further dimmed. Most world order thinking today is less inclined to rely exclusively on legal structures. It is also less uncompromising in its interpretation of disarmament, sometimes permitting residual national forces of a "strictly" defensive nature.

The McCloy-Zorin Agreements provide the precedent for a number of the most recent proposals for comprehensive disarmament. Negotiated over a three-month period in 1961, the principles would have eliminated not only all nuclear weapons but all national military establishments. Modifying and expanding upon this precedent, Marcus Raskin has drafted a "Program Treaty for Security and General Disarmament." His treaty proposes the disarmament of all nuclear and conventional armed forces (except those deemed essential for "internal order") in three five-year phases between 1985 and the year 2000. The governing instrument for this process is to be an International Disarmament Organization distinct from but related to the United Nations. While the Clark-Sohn proposal and others through the years have vested a residual component of nuclear weapons in the armory of a global peacekeeping authority, Raskin's proposal expressly forbids the possession of weapons of mass destruction and terror by any body, national or global. In addition, he proposes the adoption by each nation of a "no-surrender clause . . . which makes it a domestic crime to surrender to an aggressor nation"[2] and a Hippocratic oath for scientists and engineers "which abjures them from doing research, development, and experimental work on weapons of mass destruction."[3]

## Confining the Military to Defense

A second approach to comprehensive disarmament has been suggested by Randall Forsberg, author of the original Freeze proposal. She reasons that "by gradually confining the role of conventional military forces to defense, more and more narrowly defined, we can move safely toward a world in which conventional forces are limited to short-range, defensive armaments, in which international institutions provide an effective nonviolent means of resolving conflicts, and in which nuclear weapons can be abolished."[4] She emphasizes an incremental approach, "a series of gradual, clearly demarcated steps each of which creates a plateau of military, political, and technological stability that can be maintained for years or perhaps even decades. At each stage of the process, we must eliminate the more provocative, aggressive, or escalatory aspects of armaments, leaving the more defensive elements for later reductions."[5] Writes Forsberg:

The main functions of armed forces today are deterrence, defense, aggression, intervention, armed repression, and armed revolution. Of these, the function most compatible with achieving and maintaining a stable peace is *defense* (original emphasis). If all countries maintained military forces solely for the purpose of defending their national territory, only conventional short-range forces that provide air, coastal, and border defense would be needed. Aggression, intervention, and armed repression would then cease. Without armed repression, there would be no need for armed revolution. And without aggression, intervention, repression, and revolution, war would never be initiated. . . . Thus, national defense, defined in the narrowest and strictest sense, is entirely compatible with those changes in attitudes that are required to permit movement toward a disarmed world.[6]

## Qualitative Disarmament: Shedding the Offense

Forsberg's proposal, and others like it,[7] bear a distinct resemblance to the principle of "qualitative disarmament" introduced and exhaustively considered during the great Geneva Disarmament Conference of 1932-33 and subsequently forgotten. First proposed by Britain's Lord Robert Cecil (with technical advice from the great military strategist, B.H. Liddell Hart), the principle urged that nations agree "to decrease the offensive power of armaments, while leaving defensive power untouched . . . (for) anything which diminishes the power of aggression proportionately to the power of defense necessarily increases the safety of the world."[8] The concept was later adopted by the United States as the basis of its own set of proposals, set forth first by Herbert Hoover and later endorsed by FDR. Wrote Roosevelt in May, 1933: "If all nations will agree wholly to eliminate from possession and use weapons which make possible a successful attack, defenses automatically will become impregnable, and the frontiers and independence of every nation will become secure. The ultimate objective of the Disarmament Conference must be the complete elimination of all offensive weapons."[9]

> *If ambiguity lingers in the great gray middle of the arsenals, there are many clearly in the realms of black and white as well and the elimination of even just the darkest among them would likely make for a more stable world.*

For a time it appeared that these proposals held promise of achieving a consensus, but much energy was lost in the effort to distinguish between offensive and defensive weaponry and the entire conference was eventually upstaged by the emergence of Hitler and Germany's withdrawal from the proceedings. Now, of course, it is a far more difficult task, both to get nations to agree and to select from among the immensely greater variety of weapons now available those few that are not easily employed for attack. The dual-capable nature of so much hardware has made such distinctions highly problematical. But if ambiguity lingers in the great gray middle of the arsenals, there are many clearly in the realms of black and white as well and the elimination of even just the darkest among them would likely make for a more stable world. Most importantly, such proposals do not appear to require that we reinvent the political universe or that nations place great trust in one another. Leaving national sovereignty for the moment intact, they simply seek to curtail its most destructive expressions.

## Weaponless Deterrence

In his second major contribution to the nuclear debate, Jonathan Schell proposes a "deliberate policy" of "weaponless deterrence." Arguing that nuclear weapons have already "spoiled war" for the actual fighting, Schell proposes that we build on the better side of the precarious truce of our present "deterred state" by agreeing together to abolish nuclear weapons in the knowledge that any transgressor to the agreement would face a certain, though delayed, retaliatory strike by his victim. "Today," writes Schell, "missile deters missile, bomber deters bomber, submarine deters submarine. Under what we might call weaponless deterrence, factory would deter factory, blueprint would deter blueprint, equation would deter equation. . . . The knowledge of how to rebuild the weapons is just the thing that would make abolition *possible* (original emphasis), because it would keep deterrence in force." [10]

Nations would . . . agree, in effect, to drop their swords from their hands and lift their shields toward one another instead. . . . In keeping with the defensive aim of the agreement as a whole, these forces would, to whatever extent this was technically possible, be deployed and armed in a defensive mode. . . . Moreover, as the years passed after the signing of the agreement the superiority of the defense would be likely to increase, because defensive weapons would continue to be openly developed, tested, and deployed, while offensive weapons could not be. Therefore—probably as a separate, third provision of the agreement—anti-nuclear defensive forces would be permitted. [11]

## Unilateral Renunciation

All these proposals for disarmament require negotiation and mutual agreement. But the pathetic record of past negotiations has led many observers to conclude that in the absence of decisive independent action to initiate the necessary momentum, negotiations will remain stalled in mutual suspicion and irrelevance. There has thus grown up a small corpus of literature speculating on a coordinated set of policies that might be undertaken by one nation alone to initiate forward momentum towards disarmament. The first and most radical of these proposals advocates unilateral (nuclear) disarmament, the case for which W.H. Ferry's *A Farewell to Arms* remains the fullest expression.[12] More recently, Freeman Dyson has given attention to this option as one among several possibilities, concluding that "unilateral disarmament is not by itself a sufficient basis for a foreign policy. It needs to be supplemented by a concept stating clearly what we are to do after we have disarmed, if we are confronted by hostile powers making unacceptable demands."[13] He suggests (without fully endorsing) the possibility of **nonnuclear resistance**, a deliberate independent renunciation of the nuclear option in favor of an increased reliance on technologies and strategies of non-aggressive defense. He then seeks to envision a circumstance in which Americans could persuade themselves to kick the nuclear habit, requiring as much a psychological as a strategic shift in thinking:

It is conceivable that a new generation of military leaders will arise, determined to heal the rift which weapons of mass murder have interposed between our armed forces and our idealistic and intelligent young people. It is

conceivable that the military establishment will
itself decide that a shift to a non-nuclear strategy is required, in order to restore honor and
self-respect to the ancient profession of soldier-
ing. If our leading soldiers were convinced, as
most of the great soldiers of the past were convinced, that high morale and a sense of purpose are more essential ingredients of military
strength than big bombs, then a shift of United
States strategy to non-nuclear resistance is by
no means inconceivable.[14]

## Independent Initiatives: GRIT

Both of these appeals, the first ethical, the second sen-
timental and strategic, commit the United States to complete independent renunciation of nuclear weapons.
Others, cognizant of profound public discomfort with
such an idea, have urged that the United States undertake
a conscious **initiative strategy** that moves toward disarmament by a calculated series of steps each of which is
designed to build momentum for reciprocation. "The initiatives approach," writes Robert Woito, a participant in
the American Initiatives Project of the World Without
War Council, "rejects yielding to an opponent's will but
does grant some validity to an opponent's claim. It does
not seek the opponent's destruction. . . . A policy of peace
initiatives does not wait for agreement. It pursues its

purposes by independent actions. It recognizes that any final settlement must be based on widespread consent, but that there are situations in which only independent, non-military action, taken without prior agreement, can create a situation in which agreement becomes possible."[15]

The classic treatment of the initiative strategy is psychologist Charles Osgood's GRIT (Graduated Reciprocation In Tension-Reduction). First proposed in 1962 in a brief book entitled *An Alternative to War and Surrender*, the GRIT strategy utilizes a shrewd understanding of human motivations to generate an "arms race in reverse," "a graduated and reciprocated, unilaterally initiated, tension-decreasing system" to replace the tension-*increasing* system we call the arms race. Osgood's plan affirmed nuclear deterrence, but in a role far more circumscribed than most others of his time, advocating that we "retain only the minimum nuclear capacity required for sufficient deterrence (and this only temporarily) and that we. . . . gradually reduce our conventional forces by reciprocated initiatives to transfer to the United Nations."[16]

## Stipulations for GRIT

Using this "temporary" deterrent as a "security base from which to take limited risks in the direction of reducing tensions," Osgood specifies a number of ground rules for his strategy. Unilateral initiatives must, he says:

1. be graduated in risk according to the degree of reciprocation obtained from opponents;
2. be diversified in nature, both as to sphere of action and as to geographical locus of application. . . . cultural, scientific, economic, political, legal, as well as disarmament initiatives;
3. represent a sincere intent to reduce and control international tensions. If we are really *not* sincere . . . then this will soon become apparent to both allies and enemies alike; our unilateral initiatives will be reacted to on these terms, and nothing will be accomplished but an intensification of the cold war;
4. be announced publicly . . . before their execution and identified as part of a deliberate policy of reducing and controlling tensions; and they should include an explicit invitation to reciprocation in some form;
5. be continued over a considerable time period, regardless of immediate reciprocation or events of a tension-increasing nature elsewhere;
6. prior to announcement, unilateral initiatives must be unpredictable by an opponent as to their sphere, locus, and time of execution.[17]

Osgood emphasized that although the goal is the same as in negotiated disarmament, GRIT "is more like courtship than marriage, more like a conversation than a prayer. Rather than marching in unison, the players of GRIT move in complicated steps of their own, each keeping his eyes on the moves of the other, and leading or following, now one, now the other."[18]

## The Kennedy Experiment

Not long after Osgood's book was published, the Kennedy Administration engaged in a brief series of initiatives that appeared to confirm the validity of Osgood's theory. Shaken, perhaps, by the previous autumn's Cuban Missile Crisis, President Kennedy announced, in a now famous "Strategy for Peace" speech at the American University, a unilateral U.S. moratorium on atmospheric nuclear testing. The Soviet response was immediate: five days after Kennedy's speech, Premier Khruschev ordered a halt to the production of strategic bombers. Following the American example, the Soviets agreed not to test weapons in the atmosphere while a treaty to the same effect was being negotiated. Soviet and American negotiators reached agreement on the installation of a "hotline" between them within ten days of Kennedy's initiatory speech.

Many of the dozens of gestures proferred during this sudden thaw in superpower relations were more of a psychological than a strategic importance. Neither party yielded anything that would foreclose future options. Yet on the psychological level (which is of no small significance in such matters), something quite extraordinary occurred—so extraordinary, in fact, that the very pace of events apparently frightened both NATO allies and certain sectors of the domestic American polity.

By autumn the peace race began to stall. "The reasons were many," wrote sociologist Amitai Etzioni, who made a thorough study of what he called "the Kennedy Experiment." The Administration felt that the psychological mood in the West was getting out of hand, with hopes and expectations for more Soviet-American measures running too high; allies, especially West Germany, objected more and more bitterly; and the pre-election year began, in which the Administration seemed not to desire additional accommodations. The present *posture* [original emphasis] seemed best for domestic purposes. There had been some promising signs for those who favored disarmament, and no matters of grave enough importance were involved that even if it all went sour—if the Soviets resumed testing, orbited bombs, etc.—no credible 'appeasement' charge could be made by the Republicans."[19]

## Soviet Initiatives

Indeed, it appears from Etzioni's analysis that the problem was not that the initiatives failed but that they succeeded too well: in the popular and insightful aphorism, "nothing fails like success." "While the warnings of the critics were not realized," wrote Etzioni, "a danger that seems not to have been anticipated by the United States government did materialize: The Russians responded not just by reciprocating American initiatives but by offering some initiatives of their own, in the spirit of the detente. Washington was put on the spot: it had to reciprocate if it were not to weaken the new spirit, but it could lose control of the experiment."[20] Whether Kennedy was acting with Osgood's strategy in mind is still not clear. McGeorge Bundy reports that as Kennedy's national security adviser, he knew nothing of GRIT while in office and only recently learned of it. Kennedy evidently had only the first step in mind and was thus carried forward to subsequent initiatives largely on the spontaneous momentum of the initiative process.

Although Osgood included in his proposal a substantial research agenda for future inquiry, few others have taken up the questions he posed or sought to test and refine his strategy. Herbert Scoville once suggested a policy of "RUR" (Reciprocal Unilateral Restraint), dealing mostly with the hardware of superpower arsenals. More recently, Franklin Long has renewed consideration of the strategy,[21] which, quoting Thomas Schelling, he classifies as a variety of "tacit bargaining": "The problem is to develop a modus vivendi when one or both parties either cannot or will not negotiate explicitly, or when neither would trust the other with respect to any agreement explicitly reached."[22]

Similarly, Louis Kriesberg, researching the efficacy of what he calls "non-coercive inducements," concludes that while they cannot wholly replace negative sanctions, they may have a larger role to play than they have thus far. "It must be recognized, in dealing with international affairs," he writes, "that adversaries can influence each other very little. Coercion, too, has circumscribed effectiveness."[23]

## Warming the Weather

In conclusion, we must reluctantly admit that disarmament by negotiated agreement is a "non-starter": that is, it does not possess a momentum of its own. It requires the commitment, persistence and initiative of at least one party and at least a modicum of self-interest in both. Disarmament may be more an end than a means, the product of an improved relationship rather than its creator. "The trouble with disarmament," writes Salvador de Madariaga, veteran of many early negotiations, "was (and still is) that the problem of war is tackled upside down and at the wrong end. Nations don't distrust each other because they are armed; they are armed because they distrust each other. And therefore to want disarmament before a minimum of common agreement on fundamentals is as absurd as to want people to go undressed in winter. Let the weather be warm, and people will discard their clothes readily and without committees to tell them how to undress."[24]

"Warming the weather" by means of a sustained and comprehensive policy of independent initiatives might just improve the climate sufficiently over time (albeit very gradually) that the weaponry itself will become anachronistic, secondary to other, more profitable aspects of the relationship.

# NONVIOLENCE:
## Strengths of the Weak

> *"The potential of nonviolence is enormous. . . . In the end it could be as important as nuclear fission."*[1]
>
> – THOMAS SCHELLING

In its myriad and mostly unrecognized variety, nonviolent action likely has more than any other tradition or school of thought to offer toward the resolution of the nuclear conundrum. Yet by comparison with the warehouses of research and analysis devoted to the violent resolution of conflict, the literature of nonviolence is as a blade of grass in a field of thistles. Why it has been so thoroughly neglected by both scholars and a larger public is a question worthy of study in itself. Perhaps the fact that the very word is a double negative serves to indicate how much it remains in the shadow of what most people still believe to be a fundamentally more assertive and effective mode of behavior.

This pale imagery of nonviolence is further diminished by the mistaken impression that nonviolence is an ascetic practice appropriate only to saints and martyrs and quite beyond the capacities or inclinations of more mortal folk. Yet in the great majority of cases in which nonviolent action has been undertaken by large numbers of people in recent years—in the American South during the civil rights movement, in Czechoslovakia during the Prague Spring, in Iran in the early stages of the Revolution, in Poland's Solidarity movement, and now in the Philippines—the raw material was not anointed. These were and are ordinary human beings with ordinary capacities for self-restraint. Nonviolent action is anything but arcane. It is in fact so routine in many of its forms that we simply fail to notice our reliance on it.

## Strategic Nonviolence: Civilian-Based Defense

Nonviolent defense has been under development in a small but determined community of researchers scattered across the planet for about twenty-five years now. The acknowledged dean of this school in diaspora is Gene Sharp, whose Program on Nonviolent Sanctions in the Center for International Affairs at Harvard is the largest (and perhaps the only) project of its kind in the world today relating the strategies of nonviolence to the defense of nations. Others who began their professional lives exploring the possibilities of nonviolence have since despaired at the apparent impossibility of gaining broad acceptance of the strategy and have passed on to the more compromising tactics of alternative military defense. Sharp, on the contrary, has remained steadfast in his insistence that nonviolence is above all a practical strategy applicable to ordinary mortals and requiring no special faith in a higher order of being. In the schism between those who would take on nonviolence as an ideology and a way of life and those who would use it as a technique to accomplish specified tasks, Sharp comes down firmly in the second camp, and in fact defines it.

> *Nonviolent action is anything but arcane. It is in fact so routine in many of its forms that we simply fail to notice our reliance on it.*

The theoretical and operative basis of "civilian-based defense" (Sharp's term for nonviolent national defense) is the insight that power derives not, as so many people believe, from the barrel of a gun but from the consent or acquiescence of the governed:

One can see the power of a government as
emitted from the few who stand at the pinna-
cle of command. Or one can see that power, in
all governments, as continually rising from
many parts of the society. One can also see
power as self-perpetuating, durable, not easily
or quickly controlled or destroyed. Or political
power can be viewed as fragile, always dependent for its strength and existence upon a re-
plenishment of its sources by the cooperation
of a multitude of institutions and people—cooperation which may or may not continue.
Nonviolent action is based on the second of
these views. . . .[2]

By the withdrawal of that consent and cooperation a
people with sufficient unity of purpose and wholly without force of arms can repel an invader, even (or perhaps
most of all) in cases where resort to arms would have
produced catastrophic consequences. Civilian-based defense cannot defend geographical borders in the sense
we are accustomed to believing military defense is designed to do. But in an age of missile weaponry, even
hardware will not shield borders from penetration. The
strength of nonviolent defense inheres in its capacity for
ceaseless resistance, spoiling the spoils of war, depriving
the aggressor of his anticipated fruits of victory. Potential
aggressors thus face the daunting prospect of a low-grade
struggle without end. "There are no white flags of surrender in civilian-based defense," writes Sharp.[3]

## Crossroads Defense

George Kennan, speaking in another context a quarter century ago of a non-nuclear but not nonviolent defense for Western Europe, expressed the tone and stance most appropriate to a civilian-based resistance. The strategy he advocated would not attempt the defense of the borders of the nation. . .

but rather its defense at every village cross-
road. The purpose would be to place the country in a position where it could face the
Kremlin and say to it: 'Look here, you may be
able to overrun us, if you are unwise enough to
attempt it, but you will have a small profit
from it; we are in a position to assure that not
a single Communist or other person likely to
perform your political business will be available
to you for this purpose; you will find here no
adequate nucleus of a puppet regime; on the
contrary, you will be faced with the united and
organized hostility of an entire nation; your
stay among us will not be a happy one; we will
make you pay bitterly for every day of it; and
it will be without favorable long-term prospects.'[4]

## Political Jiu-Jitsu

Meeting violence with nonviolence is not, in Sharp's analysis, a passive response or an ethical renunciation of power but a brilliant strategic maneuver which shrewdly declines to meet the aggressor on his own terms (where he is strongest), but chooses instead to shift the ground of battle and the weapons themselves to that position where the defender himself is strongest. In this sense, civilian-based defense is a highly creative and initiatory strategy, far more so than are the more conventional defensive military postures. In radically shifting the terms of the struggle, in responding to attack not by a most predictable counter-attack nor by craven acquiescence but by a stubborn refusal to recognize and accept alien authority, civilian-based defense makes use of what Sharp calls "political jiu-jitsu":

This willingness to persist despite repression produces political jiu-jitsu. That is, the government's supposed greater power is made ineffective and turned to its own disadvantage. The repression of nonviolent people tends to alienate sympathy and support for the government—among those who might join the resistance, the government's usual supporters, and throughout the world—as the regime is seen as dependent upon, and willing to use, naked,

brutal violence against nonviolent human
beings. This may lead to increased numbers of
people becoming determined to resist such a
system. . . . Nonviolent technique applied
against a violent opponent uses the opponent's
'strength' . . . to upset his balance and contribute to his own defeat. This is not simply because of the novelty of nonviolent action,
which with the spread of the technique is already wearing off, but because of the inherent
nature of the technique itself.[5]

## Social Defense: European Studies

In various forms and under various names, nonviolent
defense has been given consideration during the past two
decades in both Western Europe and North America. In
Sweden, Denmark, and Holland, small-scale feasibility
studies have been sponsored by mildly sympathetic governments, although always at a level of funding far below
the requested sums; and the West German Green Party,
like a number of alternative parties in European parlia-
ments, has endorsed a policy of "social defense" (nonviolent defense by the entire society) to supplant
conventional armed defense. Even the French government, hardly inclined toward the renunciation of armed
force of any kind, has commissioned a limited study of
the possible usefulness of nonviolent defense.

A recently released Swedish study sternly forbids consideration of any defense based wholly on nonviolent strategies but grants (with apparent reluctance) that they may be useful as a supplement to existing military forms. The governmental commission's working assumptions were two: "Civilian defence cannot form an alternative to the Swedish military defense. 2. The task is an investigation only of the conceivable situation that regular military defense can no longer be carried out." And further: "Refraining from a military defence within the limits of a total defence would probably be considered lack of will to vindicate our independence."[6] The Swedish commission does not appear to anticipate a gradual substitution of one defense policy for the other.

In the tone and stance of the Swedish report, one senses a kind of territorial imperative at work, a reluctance on the part of the Ministry of Defence (to whom it was submitted) to allow the idea to gain a foothold from which it might later seek to gain a wider berth. This hesitation reflects the irony that those being asked to consider the change—the armed forces—stand to lose their jobs by the maneuver. A policy that appears to threaten both the livelihood and identity of a central and substantial segment of the population, while abolishing a profession still highly revered among a considerable public, stands little chance of being taken seriously in the immediate term.

# Disarmies: The Unarmed Forces

It may thus be worth considering whether those of us advocating nonviolent defense strategies should be making use of this immense social institution, the armed forces, in our conversion plans. Their stated purpose, contrary to their actual effect, is, after all, to prevent harm. Gene Keyes, a Canadian theorist of "strategic nonviolent defense," has written an intriguing proposal for an unarmed military service:

Let us postulate "disarmies" . . . In all cases, the essential duty of these unarmed services would be: ever to give life, never to take it . . . There are hundreds of political/military possibilities. The United Nations is a logical birthplace for unarmed forces, but just for the sake of argument, we could depict them established by Costa Rica or Canada, the North Atlantic Treaty Organization or the Nordic Council, the U.S. or Yugoslavia, the Irish Republican Army or Mongolia, Solidarity or Somalia. . . . They would be a social invention, a political instrument in a world still afflicted by deadly power conflicts, occasional genocide, structural violence, natural disasters, ecological trauma, nuclear roulette, and the military habits of a millennium. Unarmed forces might well be ac-

quired as a deliberate initiative, or through un-
foreseen mutation, by polities that had the
vision or serendipity to do so.[7]

Keyes identifies ten "military missions" for these unarmed forces:

1.    **Rescue action**: "The employment of military ca-
      pability for saving lives and setting up disaster
      relief in times of natural or manmade catastro-
      phe."
2.    **Civic action**: "for social service projects such as
      local construction, farming, public health, trans-
      portation, education, communication, conserva-
      tion, community development, and the like."
3.    **Colossal action**: "The employment of military ca-
      pability, especially logistic, in constructive social
      enterprises of enormous magnitude, possibly re-
      quiring ships in the thousands, aircraft in the tens
      of thousands, personnel in the hundreds of mil-
      lions, and dollars in the hundreds of billions per
      year."
4.    **Friendly persuasion**: "The use or display of non-
      violent military force during normal or crisis pe-
      riods for such purposes as goodwill, deterrence,
      show of strength, propaganda, hostage deploy-
      ment, and political, psychological or economic
      warfare; by means such as public and joint ma-
      neuvers, and the delivery of messages, food, equip-
      ment, gifts, or hostages, whether requested or
      not."

5.  **Guerrilla action**: "Aggressive and unconventional initiatives by irregular but disciplined unarmed forces waging a revolutionary and/or defensive struggle against a more powerful opponent."

6.  **Police action**: "for law enforcement, peace observation, and peacekeeping duties, in situations beyond the control of local authority."

7.  **Buffer action**: "The deployment of unarmed military force between belligerents before, during, or after active hostilities."

8.  **Defense**: "This sight of marching, and probably uniformed, nonviolent brigades might give the citizens a sense of security. To the average citizen a nonviolent army of professional resistance fighters would personify the will to resist and give him the assurance that they would in any event do their job and not leave him in the lurch. The existence of a fearless nonviolent army, which would offer resistance to the last man, might act as a stronger warning to the potential invader than an invisible system of resistance cells."[8]

9.  **Expeditionary action**: "An unarmed military mission across national boundaries. . . . defense of another nation on its own territory, or temporary intervention in restraint of flagrant injustice, oppression, invasion or genocide."

10. **Nonviolent invasion**: "Given a substantial array of unarmed forces, a Just War need no longer be a moral Frankenstein but instead a legitimate, humane, and essential response by a larger com-

munity of nations when an entire people are in danger."[9]

Keyes' social inventions extend nonviolent action into an entire second realm of activity beyond its traditional non-cooperation. While Gene Sharp and most other theorists of nonviolent defense use nonviolence as a mode of resistance, Keyes suggests it as a mode of reconstruction, employing the very institution we have so long resisted to perform genuinely useful tasks. Audacious and improbable as it seems, the proposal bears the considerable merit of preserving both the jobs and identities of the "uniformed services," albeit while assigning them a much altered set of functions.

Of course one could not expect the transformation to occur all at once, and perhaps not even consciously in its earlier phases. Nations may find themselves increasingly called upon to meet natural emergencies of supranational scale and may decide to employ the facilities of their armed services to complete the tasks, as is done routinely with the National Guard in the case of floods. The harnessing of this venerable but much abused institution to address what psychologists call "superordinate goals"— stemming famine in one instance, reclaiming and reforesting desertified land in another—could, given the right "packaging," become one of the better games than war that social inventor Robert Fuller believes we need.[10]

# Nuclear Blackmail: Facing Down the Threat

Excellent as are the proposals of both Genes, neither they nor most other theorists of nonviolent defense choose to deal directly with that eventuality most dreaded by the strategists of nuclear deterrence: nuclear blackmail. The bottom line, say the nuclear strategists, is no longer a land invasion that can be repelled by conventional armed force or resisted by nonviolence, but the naked threat of nuclear attack, against which both strategies are impotent and only a counter-threat will deter.

At least a few theorists have in fact attempted to refute this assumption and to address the threat of nuclear blackmail entirely by nonviolent action. The first and in some respects still most compelling argument for unarmed defiance of nuclear threats came from Commander Sir Stephen King-Hall, son and grandson of British admirals and himself a high naval officer. In an extraordinary book published a quarter century ago (*Defence in the Nuclear Age*), he proposed that Britain independently renounce not only its nuclear weapons but also the greater share of its non-nuclear armed force and rely instead on its unarmed will to resist domination—and its capacity to carry the political battle back to the opponent by assertively propagating its own ideas to the audience of the world community. What is most persuasive in King-Hall's proposal is its appeal to the heroic impulse, a key psychological element in the continuing attraction of war and a factor often neglected in alternative defense theories:

It is a fascinating exercise of imagination to
picture a besieged Britain living on its own resources, the centre of world attention, the min-
ers performing prodigies of output, the
agricultural community extracting every ounce
of food from our soil, the whole nation on a
basic food, fuel and clothing ration and basic
wage, party politics forgotten and a renaissance
of national purpose and unity far exceeding
those stirring days (never to be forgotten by
those who participated in them), when Great
Britain stood alone at Dunkirk.[11]

Although King-Hall's proposal aroused great conster-
nation and controversy at the time of its publication and
has since languished on library shelves, it earned the
notice and praise of the greatest of twentieth-century
military strategists, Sir Basil Liddell Hart. "It is remarkable, and deeply significant," he wrote, "that a man so
combative by temperament and heredity should become
a leading advocate of nonviolent resistance. Moreover,
events have proved his foresight about the trend of warfare. While the practicability of his proposals can be ques-
tioned, his argument presents a challenge which deserves
the fullest consideration—and cannot be ignored. . . .
Even on practical grounds there is a stronger case for
nonviolence than is generally realized."[12]

More recently, peace researcher Richard Fogg has sought to focus attention once again on this most improbable and yet most promising of strategies. Describing a policy of "nonmilitary defense against nuclear threateners and attackers," Fogg identifies four sources of potential leverage:

1. **international ostracism**: "a superforce . . . disapproval, no trade except for a few essentials, practically no attention in the media—withdrawal of virtually everything."
2. **nonviolent coup d'etat**: "to divide the opposition enough that some of its leaders would depose those responsible for the crisis."
3. **removing injustices**: achieving fair settlements of outstanding disputes between adversaries so that force becomes unnecessary.
4. **civilian-based defense**: "massive nonviolent actions prepared by governments."[13]

As is often the case, it is George Kennan, speaking in another context, who best expresses the kind of determination that would be vital to a wholly nonviolent defiance of nuclear blackmail. What can a country without nuclear weapons do, he was asked, when threatened by a country with nuclear weapons? He replied:

Stalin said the nuclear weapon is something with which you frighten people with weak nerves. He could not have been more right.

No one in his right senses would yield to any such thing as nuclear blackmail. In the first place, it would be most unlikely (as is the case with most forms of blackmail) that the threat would be made good if one defied it. Secondly, there would be no point in yielding to it. Any regime that has not taken leave of its senses would reject the nuclear threat.

"Why in the world should we give in to this," it would argue. "If we do what you want us to do today in the name of this threat, what are you going to ask us to do tomorrow? There is no end to this process. If what you want us to do is to part with our independence, you will have to find others to do your work for you, and that means that you will have to take ultimate responsibility for running this country. We are not going to be the people to turn this government into an instrument of your power." No one would give in to this kind of pressure; nor does anybody use this kind of blackmail. Great governments do not behave that way.[14]

## Are We Brave Enough?

Freeman Dyson, eclectic in his consideration of all possibilities, poses the question most directly and leaves the answer open:

Sooner or later, everybody who thinks seriously about the meaning of nuclear weapons and nuclear war must face the question whether nonviolence is or is not a practical alternative to the path we are now following. Is nonviolence a possible basis for the foreign policy of a great country like the United States? Or is it only a private escape route available to religious minorities who are protected by a majority willing to fight for their lives? I do not know the answers to these questions. I do not think that anybody knows the answers. ... It would take a whole country of people standing together with extraordinary courage and extraordinary discipline.

Can we find such a country in the world as it is today? Perhaps we can, among countries which are small and homogeneous and possess a long tradition of quiet resistance to oppression. But how about the United States? Can we conceive of the population of the United States standing together in brotherhood and self-sacrifice like the villagers of Le Chambon? It is difficult to imagine any circumstances which would make this possible. But history teaches us that many things which were once unimaginable nevertheless came to pass.[15]

## QUESTIONS:

1.    Nonviolence has traditionally been understood to be a passive response to a more fundamental original act which sets the tone and terms of the struggle. Do we need to develop a more assertive understanding of nonviolence that emphasizes its capacity to initiate action and sustain the initiative, its capacity to redefine the terms of struggle, to move and resettle the argument on ground where it is itself strongest?

2.    The term, nonviolence, is a double negative. Is there any other word that would express the concept in terms of what it is rather than what it is not?

3.    It has frequently been argued that civilian-based defense might possibly succeed in a small, homogeneous society beyond the strategic battlegrounds of the great powers but not in a highly fractionated society committed to the polarities of the East-West power struggle. Has CBD any relevance to the defense of the United States or NATO nations? To non-NATO nations in Western Europe? What is its relevance to Eastern Europe, where (in Poland and Czechoslovakia) nonviolent resistance has taken its most advanced forms?

4.  Can nonviolent defense be integrated with a traditional or reformed military defense without placing the nonviolent element at risk?

5.  Does the successful use of nonviolent techniques and strategies require a moral commitment to the concept?

6.  What would be the nature of a nonviolent defense against nuclear threats? What would be the likely response from a determined aggressor?

7.  Why is nonviolence popularly thought to be a strategy of the weak? How can this perception be altered?

8.  Can large military establishments be expected to entertain seriously a strategy and policy that puts them out of a job?

9.  What roles have nonviolent strategies to play in pressuring reluctant governments on both sides of the divide to come to agreement on the dismantling of nuclear weapons? What place have transnational actions?

10. Nonviolence is most often understood and expressed as a strategy of resistance. Should it also be understood as a strategy of affirmation and creation, inventing its own alternative institutions and patterns of behavior to supplant those it rejects?

11. Does successful nonviolent action really require extraordinary expressions of brotherhood and self-sacrifice or can it succeed as well by pure cussedness and ungovernability?

# PEACE RESEARCH:
## Beyond "Permanent Pre-Hostilities"

*"The fact that we have had a world of
unstable peace at best for thousands of
years does not mean that it is something
that has to go on forever. It is possible
to have a profound though frequently
imperceptible shift in the nature of the
system which carries us, as it were, over
a kind of watershed into a very different social landscape."*[1]

– KENNETH BOULDING

Nearly all that has been written under the rubric of peace
research and conflict resolution bears upon the question
of how to move beyond the Bomb. What are the causes
of peace, its essential conditions and components? How
can it be brought into being and then sustained? From
one point of view nearly all the fields of inquiry we have
already reviewed ask similar questions in one or another
more specific context. I will make no pretense of review-

ing the range of useful studies in this field; there are far too many and I know too few of them. I will confine myself here to just a few authors and themes which strike me as particularly insightful in introducing the notion of a peace "system" to replace the war system that currently governs a large portion of global politics.

## Positive and Negative Peace

"Peace is not merely the absence of war," writes Herbert Kelman, marking a distinction between "negative" and "positive" peace,

but the maintenance of a state of affairs that can be defined in positive terms. Thus, one cannot very well describe as peaceful a world that is constantly on the brink of war and in which war is avoided only by the threat of nuclear annihilation or by the violent repression of discontented elements. Positive peace does not imply an ideal, utopian situation, but merely a livable one—a world in which peace is probable. . . . Peace does not imply the absence of conflict. Some degree of conflict is an inevitable and often desirable process in any social system. . . . The problem is not to avoid conflict, but to prevent it from turning into mass destruction.[2]

These twin insights, both well-accepted premises in the peace research community, have not yet been fully understood by either the larger peace movement or the greater society beyond. The peace movement currently focuses the bulk of its efforts on preventing the worst, believing it is the most they can hope for (which may be true) and viewing these defensive efforts as the best means of deterring calamity. Both the peace movement and the larger public, meanwhile, generally imagine peace in terms so rarefied and unblemished by ordinary reality, that they may fail to notice its presence when it is already in the very room with them. Perhaps this is not peace in the august sense in which we usually imagine it, but what Kenneth Boulding calls "non-conflict":

Because of the dramatic qualities of conflict we fall easily into what I have called the 'dramatic fallacy,' that overestimates the importance of the dramatic simply because it is visible and underestimates the importance of the great, quiet invisible changes that go on underneath. It is the quiet people, the farmers and the manufacturers, the businessmen and bankers, the inventors and innovators and those who imitate the innovation who really bring about the great cumulative changes in the state of the world.[3]

What these comments suggest to me is that we may not know yet just what peace is, as an actual experience, and so we know even less of how to go about getting or making it. Captive to Boulding's "dramatic fallacy," we may be looking past peace because its face is so often plain. We have as yet so dim an impression of its shapes and expressions that we refer to it more often in terms of what it is not than of what it is, as the term and concept of "nonviolence" reflect. Herbert Kelman suggests that we need to shift our thinking from a medical model of peace research, based on the prevention of the "war disease," to a "public health model" based on a comprehensive and integrated understanding of political and social well-being.[4]

We need also, of course, to believe that a healthy culture and society are in fact possible. The term, "robust," mentioned in other contexts by both Freeman Dyson ("a robust strategic concept") and Dietrich Fischer ("robust systems of international security") seems most appropriate to describe the kind of health one would hope for— a peace resilient enough to stand persistent abuse and neglect and still function after a fashion, a peace broadly enough based among both leaders and commoners that it runs counter to their interests to disturb it, a sometimes rowdy and rollicking peace that fully expresses the profane verve of human feeling.

## Designing Peace Systems

But how do we go about translating this metaphor of

global political health into an integrated system in which each component feeds the others in a positive synergy? If the war system (described by, among others, Richard Falk and Samuel Kim),[5] operates on a perverse dynamic of reinforcing negativities, can we devise a practical peace system that makes use of an equally potent but more benign dynamic? And more importantly, can we fashion it from elements already present in our political universe (even if they are as yet poorly developed) to spare us the considerable labor of reinventing the world and re-imagining human nature?

A peace system as here understood is not simply a modified war system. It is a synthesis of mutually reinforcing elements blended into an integrated system in which the machinery of war is gradually supplanted by the coordinated mechanisms of international peacekeeping and a complex web of less formal arrangements. The formal mechanisms would center around constitutionally established global organizations vested with the necessary authority and capacity to inspect and enforce international law and to settle disputes without resort to armed force. Before relinquishing the unlimited right to possess and develop the hardware of unilateral defense, governments and peoples will both need to feel fully assured that their security can be better guaranteed by other means. We are no more likely to succeed in persuading nations to give up their missiles than we have been in persuading American citizens to give up their handguns until we can provide both with a system of justice and a climate of safety that render them obsolete.

> *We have yet to consider what elements must be developed in an international system to channel conflict.*

Arms control as we have come to know it has no such larger understanding of its ends and means. It is a piecemeal proposition, like a set of temporary dikes hastily thrown up to stem a flood that has caught us unawares. We have not yet begun to consider the techniques of flood prevention—the construction, in advance of the flood, of a network of protective dams, the planting of shelterbelts to hold the soil. Nor have we yet considered how to make use of the enormous and potentially useful energy that comes to us now in these destructive torrents. In parallel ways, we have yet to consider what elements must be developed in an international system to channel conflict, to dissipate and divert floods of destructive emotion, what kinds of structures and shelters help hold human societies together.

## Increasing Strength, Reducing Strain

Recommending a "make-do" approach, Kenneth Boulding proposes a peace policy that "looks at the problem in terms of both reducing strain on the system and increasing its strength to resist strain, the latter depending a great deal on convention and taboo. The object is not to produce a system of infinite strength capable of resisting all strain but to simply reduce strain and increase strength and so increase the likelihood that the system will resist strain."[6]

These principles may sound somewhat abstract to the policy-oriented ear but they are well-translated into that strategic realm by both Johan Galtung and Dietrich Fischer. Both emphasize the necessity of developing the internal vigor of one's culture and economy in order to increase their strength and reduce their vulnerability. They also stress nurturing positive relationships with all those nations with whom one must do business, thus reducing the cumulative strain on the system. This kind of multi-dimensional, integrated thinking about the nature and functioning of a peace system is still somewhat new, even in the peace research community, but already it demonstrates a greater sophistication than our more prevalent models of "disease prevention."

Speculating on the nature of a peace system, Beverly Woodward notes that it "appears to require widespread, coordinated, multilateral action on a scale that we have yet to see in human affairs. . . . The institution of peace, however, should be seen mainly as a *process* rather than as an ultimate goal with static content. Peace is not some wonderful object that we can possess once certain prescribed steps have been accomplished, but a way of living and struggling that can begin now and that will have to continue (with its attendant difficulties) even after many desirable institutional changes have been achieved."[7]

Kenneth Boulding and others have observed that at this moment in the social evolution of the species, we are in a "strange limbo" in which war has largely lost its legitimacy but peace has not yet established its own as a replacement. "In the dynamics of society we see kind of a seesaw between war weariness and delegitimation and war proneness and relegitimation, but as the costs of war become more onerous one suspects that the balance of the dynamics of legitimation will be on the side of peace."[8] Others may find it hard to muster Boulding's sanguine interpretation of events but the point is still well-taken. Only when we can envision and believe the possibility of political and social health will we be able to exercise sufficient will to give it life.

## Functionalism: The Pragmatic Approach

The last word on peace systems should perhaps be left to David Mitrany, whose book, *A Working Peace System*, helped to define and establish what has come to be called **functionalism**, the pragmatic approach to peace-building. "A world society (is) more likely to grow through doing things together in workshop and marketplace than by signing pacts in chancelleries. . . ."[9] "The choice we shall have to make at every point will be between a gratifying form and the effective working of the international experiment."[10] "A constitutional pact could do little more than lay down certain elementary rights and duties for the members of the new community. The community itself will acquire a living body not through a written act of faith but through active organic development."[11]

"What would be the broad lines of such a functional organization of international activities?" he asks. "The essential principle is that activities would be selected specifically and organized separately—each according to its nature, to the conditions under which it has to operate, and to the needs of the moment. It would allow, therefore, all freedom of practical variation in the organization of the several functions, as well as in the working of a particular function as needs and conditions alter."[12]

Mitrany's functional approach, with its emphasis on what "works," would seem a world away from the constitutional and institutional approaches of Clark-Sohn and others, yet they need not be viewed as contradictory. A functioning peace system would necessarily require a panoply of formal governing institutions, but these structures would remain empty vessels unless there were also an informal interpenetration of economies and cultures. "Every activity organizing in [this] way would be a layer of peaceful life," writes Mitrany. "And a sufficient addition of them would suffuse the world with a fertile mingling of common endeavor and achievement."[13]

# ECONOMIC CONVERSION:
## Swords Into Services

Any design for demilitarizing global politics must necessarily involve a fundamental restructuring of the economies of those nations now engaged in the wholesale
manufacture of advanced offensive weaponry. A great
deal of thinking has been done in the past twenty years
or more about how this transformation might take place.
The most persistent and devoted advocate of economic
conversion research is Seymour Melman. Under his guid-
ance and inspiration, a great deal of highly detailed speculative planning has been done—yet not nearly enough.
The peculiarities of local circumstances necessitate that
each case be handled differently. It is a massive task, for
which purpose Melman recommends joint conversion
planning boards composed of both workers and management. Among the difficulties such groups would face are
the following:

1. A lack of cost consciousness in a defense industry
   with cost-plus contracts and few incentives to cut
   expenses. "The men in military work have generated a trained incapacity for minimizing cost,"

writes Melman.[1]

2.    The absence of ready functions for plant equipment in the manufacture of consumer goods. Whereas after the Second World War industrial manufacturers were able to "reconvert" quickly to those functions they had performed only four years before, many defense contractors today have been building advanced weaponry for a full generation, along lines with little immediate application to the production of useful consumer goods.

3.    In addition to industrial conversion, one must consider the problems of "individual conversion," the retraining of the great pool of engineers and technicians now engaged in the invention and production of lethal weapons. Melman proposes an "economic bill of rights for veterans of military industry" to aid in the adjustment.[2]

4.    There may be a cultural resistance among some workers to being asked to cease performing what they may believe to be a vital and prestigious line of work. Melman recalls a conversation with a Soviet weapons plant manager who, when presented with the possibility of converting his machinery to the production of consumer goods, remarked disdainfully, "What would you have us make, then? *Sausages?*"[3]

5.    Not only new jobs but new markets and products must be created to absorb the industrial and technical capacity released from weapons production. Much of this capacity is of a highly specialized

nature. Computers, rapid transit, and the development of alternative energy sources are just three among a wide variety of possible uses for this advanced technical expertise.

6.   Somehow the more fundamental needs of our domestic societies now in neglect must be met. The fact that these are often more in the realm of human services than engineering may require us to shift our educational priorities over the next generation to serve a quite different set of needs and constituencies.

7.   If the transformation were undertaken without sufficient planning and care, the economy itself might experience a severe shock—even a depression. But since disarmament on such a scale shows little signs of suddenly overwhelming us, this may prove a baroque concern.

These and many other questions will need to be answered in the course of making an orderly transition from a militarized to a demilitarized economy. But conversion plans are at least equally useful for their highly persuasive effect on the debate about whether to undertake the change at all. Since several million American workers are directly dependent on military contracts for their bread and butter, they will not likely lend their support to policies that appear to threaten that livelihood unless it can be demonstrated that their skills will be in demand elsewhere. Planning well in advance of the conversion, especially if done by the workers and managers themselves, could do much to persuade them of this possibility.

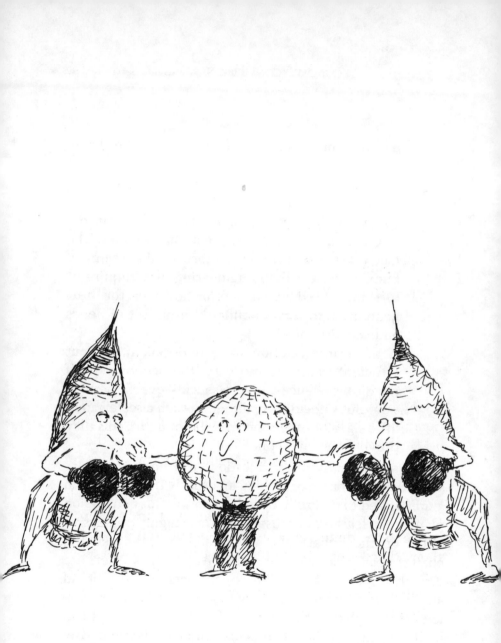

# NEGOTIATION:
## Tying Is Winning

However we go about dismantling the Bomb, it will at some point, and likely at many points, require negotiation. As it is being taught and developed at the Program on Negotiation at Harvard, negotiation is less a theory than a practice, a set of axioms and operative rules for maximizing mutual benefit in any dispute. As interpreted by Roger Fisher and William Ury in their immensely popular *Getting to Yes*, these techniques are as appropriate to the dining table as to the negotiating table, and their advice is now being tested in both places and many others as well. The core of the theory, which they call "principled negotiation" or "negotiation on the merits," is simply stated:

1.  "Separate the people from the problem. . . . Participants should come to see themselves as working side by side, attacking the problem, not each other."[1]

2.    "Focus on interests, not positions. . . . Be hard on the problem, soft on the people."[2]

3.    "Invent options for mutual gain. . . . Generate a variety of possibilities before deciding what to do. Give them a yessable proposition."[3]

4.    "Insist on using objective criteria. . . . Never yield to pressure, only to principle."[4]

Stated with such refreshing simplicity that they may appear deceptively self-evident, these principles would likely wreak a considerable transformation on the negotiating process between the superpowers even if only one of the parties applied them. They are not so much an object for further research as for further practice, on all levels of society, and their cumulative effect can only be beneficial.

> *For both the wisdom of its advice and the means of its expression, we would do well to study negotiation practice.*

What is most impressive about this body of thinking is its accessibility. Alone among the fields I have surveyed, negotiation theory has been expressed in terms that can be understood and applied by ordinary people across a vast range of circumstances. Its broad appeal is not, I think, the consequence of being any easier to comprehend than defense, disarmament, or nonviolence. It has been a conscious decision on the part of its inventors to speak simply, directly, and entertainingly, to an audience beyond its own academic discipline, to state complex truths in the simplest terms that will convey their full meaning. For both the wisdom of its advice and the means of its expression, we would do well to study negotiation practice.

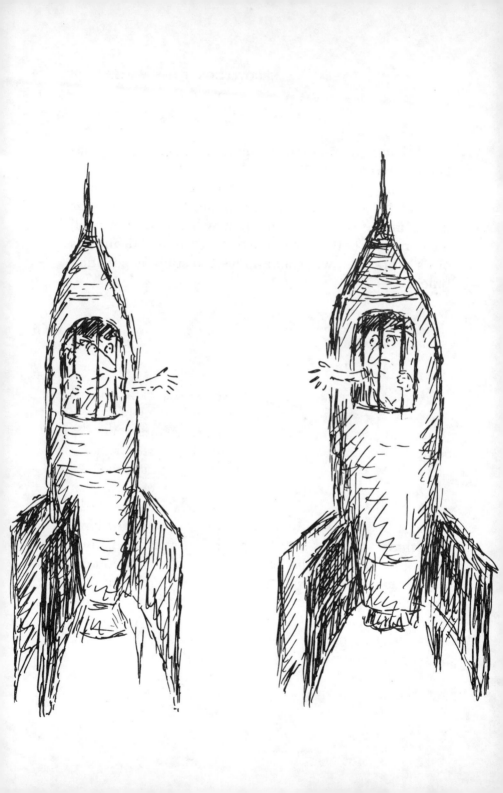

# GAME THEORY:
## Nice Guys Last Longest

First conceived as a branch of mathematics, game theory has over the years also drawn the interest of both war strategists and peace researchers. Highly adaptable to computer simulations, the structured choices can be played off against one another with a speed and degree of complexity unattainable by the use of mere verbal models. The interest of peace researchers has been sparked by a recognition that game theory might have something to tell us about both the perverse dynamics of an arms race and the benign dynamic of cooperation.

One classic conundrum that has drawn much attention from both game theorists and social psychologists has been the so-called "Prisoner's Dilemma." Two thieves working together have landed themselves in jail. Locked in separate cells, they are both presented with the following choices: "Confess and implicate the other: if he is meanwhile maintaining innocence, we shall set you

free and imprison him for five years. If neither of you
confesses, you will both get two years for lack of better
evidence. If you both confess, we have both of you, and
will give each of you a slightly mitigated four-year term."[1]

> *The most reliably winning strat-
> egy is not that of the opportunist
> defector but of the "conditional"
> cooperator.*

The terms of the deal are such that it profits one most
to betray one's partner—unless, of course, he is also be-
traying you. But it also profits you to cooperate, as long
as he also cooperates. Abstract though the game appears,
it represents a predicament not so very different from
that facing superpower rivals at the negotiating table.
The temptation is to plunge for short-term gain at your
partner's expense: a zero-sum strategy; you profit by his
loss. But recent investigations of this riddle indicate that
the most reliably winning strategy is not that of the opportunist defector but of the "conditional" cooperator.
Robert Axelrod, a University of Michigan game theorist,
recently held two public tournaments to test competing
strategies for the Prisoner's Dilemma, and his results,
published in a book entitled *The Evolution of Cooperation*,[2] indicate that, in the words of Lewis Thomas, "it is
simply not true that 'nice guys finish last'; rather, nice
guys last the longest."[3]

The winner in both tournaments was pioneer peace researcher (and long-time player of Prisoner's Dilemmas) Anatol Rapoport. Applying a simple strategy he calls "Tit for Tat," Rapoport always began by cooperating. If his partner betrayed his trust, he would also defect—but only once, after which he would once again cooperate *if* his partner cooperated. "A 'nice' strategy," notes Lewis Thomas, "but not too nice. It cooperates with cooperation, retaliates against betrayal, remembers, forgives, and can be trusted. It is also a strategy that can spread swiftly through any community of players using other strategies. A cluster of Tit for Tat strategists can defend themselves against other, hostile or aggressive players. Once established within a sea of competitors . . . it emerges as the only game in town."[4]

> *The individuals do not have to be rational: the evolutionary process allows the successful strategies to thrive, even if the players do not know why or how.*

"The main results of Cooperation Theory are encouraging," writes Axelrod. "They show that cooperation can get started by even a small cluster of individuals who are prepared to reciprocate cooperation, even in a world where no one else will cooperate. . . . But what is most interesting is how little had to be assumed about the individuals or the social setting to establish these results. The individuals do not have to be rational: the evolutionary process allows the successful strategies to thrive, even if the players do not know why or how. Nor do the players have to exchange messages or commitments: they do not need words, because their deeds speak for them. Likewise, there is no need to assume trust between the players: the use of reciprocity can be enough to make defection unproductive. Altruism is not needed: successful strategies can elicit cooperation even from an egoist. Finally, no central authority is needed: cooperation based on reciprocity can be self-policing."[5]

Peace researcher Dietrich Fischer extrapolates several lessons from the success of Tit for Tat to apply to an alternative security policy: 1. Never initiate conflict; 2. Don't passively accept negative behavior but respond immediately; 3. Don't retaliate excessively. Having made your point, return immediately to a cooperative stance. Don't escalate the conflict or lock yourself into a negative syndrome. 4. Let your strategy be simple and transparent, so that your adversary can learn to rely on your responses and act accordingly.

Cooperative behavior, the mixed-sum strategy, does in fact pay over the long term and does in fact evolve naturally out of repeated experiences with the unprofitability of betrayal. It does, at least, in the world of game theory. It probably does also in the hardball world of superpower rivalry, but so great is the fascination with short-term gain that even the likelihood of long-term loss may not deter the opportunist from grasping for a quick advantage. Still, it is a persuasive argument in favor of cooperation that its reward is not solely to be gained in heaven but here on earth as well, if only one persists long enough.

# ALTERNATIVE FUTURISM:
## Toward More Practical Utopias

*"The rise and fall of images of the future precedes or accompanies the rise and fall of cultures. As long as a society's image is positive and flourishing, the flower of a culture is in full bloom. Once the image begins to decay and lose its vitality, however, the culture does not long survive."*[1]

– FRED POLAK

When Dutch sociologist Fred Polak first made his appeal for a rebirth of a positive sense of the future, Europe was just emerging from the debris and devastation of the Second World War, an exhausted and despairing civilization. "It is scarcely possible to overestimate the extent of the tremendous spiritual reversal which has so silently taken place in our day," he wrote. "We must fully appreciate the fact that never before in the history of human civilization, as far as we know, has there been a period without any kind of positive images of the future. This in itself is already the breach in our times."[2]

Eventually, of course, a new set of hopes emerged, and a large and prosperous discipline of futurism took shape to express that hope. It was mostly a material dream, evoked by a worshipful faith in the omniscience of science and the beneficence of technology. The approaches which today dominate meetings of the World Future Society are mostly managerial in emphasis (although I am told this may be changing), planning and predicting futures that are almost straight-line projections from the present moment. "Now, nearly forty years after the war," writes Elise Boulding, "mainstream futurism has little to offer besides the technological fix. Polak asked for visions. Futurists gave blueprints."[3]

> *Out of the very bounty of technological abundance and among those best situated to benefit from it there arose a profound mistrust of all things technological.*

This servicing of the status quo gave us at least the appearance of the future it was predicting—better living through higher production and greater consumption. But behind the artist's conception of progress there emerged a new dissatisfaction, even a new despair, wholly unanticipated in the architectural plans of the futurists. Out of the very bounty of technological abundance and among those best situated to benefit from it there arose a profound mistrust of all things technological, a growing dread that our inventions were taking on a life of their own and thus threatening ours. Among a generation habituated to technical marvels there grew up an anti-technological romanticism, a yearning to escape a too perfect and too final future—or its sudden termination in holocaust. Thus it is that Fred Polak's appeal to us to revive our collective social imagination has become once again as relevant as it was a generation ago.

## Revisioning Positive Futures

There is a modest but rapidly growing literature in futurism which takes up the tasks assigned by Polak. After a season of nightmares, we are once more busy "re-visioning" positive futures. As it was essential during the past several years to finish imagining apocalypse so that we could rouse ourselves to prevent its occurrence, so it seems we must now finish imagining the better alternatives—in all the idiosyncratic detail which alone will make them real to us.

At the same time we need to accept with modesty the limitations of our predictive capacities and heed Richard Falk's injunction against "the fallacy of premature specificity." During the past decade and more, a genre of future thinking has emerged which veers away from the linear projections aimed at a technotopia and proceeds instead in a lateral direction toward a civilization both more global and more local in nature. This imagined future goes by various names—"post-industrial," "trans-industrial," "sustainable," "steady-state"—but exhibits a remarkable constancy of values and arrangements. All these visions tend toward a simplification of needs and a multiplication of choices, an enhancement of the quality of life and an acknowledgment of the finite quantity of the sources to supply it, a sense of community in place of anonymity.

> *Nuclear weapons are not a readily detachable appendage of the present system but simply the most egregious symptom of its dysfunction.*

Not all of these scenarios appear to bear directly on the shape of a future beyond the Bomb. That particular problem has not always been foremost in the minds of alternative futurists. Nor would many of those seeking to defuse the Bomb wish to encumber the cause with the baggage of a grand variety of desirable but perhaps dispensable social changes. Others believe, on the contrary, that nuclear weapons are not a readily detachable appendage of the present system but simply the most egregious symptom of its dysfunction and thus cannot be dispensed with without adopting a host of other social and institutional changes. For envisioning and specifying these changes in an attractive and integrated fashion, the literature of alternative futures, as well as its sister disciplines of alternative economics and energy, provide a mother lode of useful data and designs.

## Imaging a Weaponless World

Several years ago, sociologists Elise Boulding and Warren Ziegler devised an experimental format for imaging a world without weapons. In their workshops, participants are asked to imagine themselves thirty years hence, in the circumstance in which the change has already occurred: the weapons have in fact been dismantled. Absurd as this assumption may appear to the skeptical mind of the apparent realist, it is an essential precondition to liberating the imagination to consider new and useful possibilities. Elise Boulding explains:

The concept of a breach in time is not only a
poetic flight of fancy but an absolute necessity
if one is to free the imagination to do its work.
If one tries to work toward the future from the
present, the known realities cling like tendrils
to every new idea, smothering it with awareness of what won't work because of the way
things are. This is particularly true in the case
of visualizing a weapon-free world, because the

world is so highly armed at present that it is
almost impossible, standing in 1982, to imagine
that things could be different. The breach in
time enables the mind to overleap those local
impossibilities that loom so large in the present. There, in the new space-time, the mind
can look around and see and hear with the in-
ward eye and ear how things are in a world
that we know by declaration (there must be a
willing suspension of disbelief) has no weapons.[4]

And what does the mind see? Boulding assembles a
composite vision from the several hundred participants
who have thus far taken the workshop:

(They) see a very localist world imbued with a
strong sense of planetary consciousness. . .
more towards the rural end of the rural-urban
continuum . . . There is an audible, gentle hum
of activity in these communities. People are
visible to one another, weave in and out of
each other's lives, alternate work and play, and
see education as a life-long activity. . . . These
are not conflict-free communities, nor are they
parochial. Conflict is valued as a source of crea-
tivity, growth and development, as an important social resource. Hence the life-long
training, beginning with very young children,
in creative management of conflict. . . . International peace brigades, training in nonviolent

civilian defense for all citizens of border towns in all countries, and special cross-generation conflict resolution teams consisting of the elderly and the young, are all devices to help prevent (a return to militarism).[5]

## Historians of the Future

Following this "imaging of the totally other," the participants are asked to become historians of the "future present moment" and to trace the course of history back from the future toward the present in five-year increments. While most participants saw a period of escalating crises in the Eighties and Nineties, none envisioned a full-scale nuclear war or collapse of the social order. The change itself was seen as a "Great Turning" in which individuals and groups outside governmental structures took responsibility for crafting a peace that nations themselves seemed unable or unwilling to arrange.

Children were often pictured as taking leadership in ending the preoccupation with weaponry in a late twentieth century version of the medieval children's crusades. Nine to twelve-year-olds, or teenaged youth, travelled in teams around the world, holding international gatherings, refusing to attend school or obey parental commands as a strategy in their strug-

gle for the right to have a world to grow up
in[6]. . . . Since the knowledge to build new
weapons continued to exist in every society,
the only way to keep that knowledge from
being activated was the widespread development of social values, skills and institutional
structures which would make weapons appear
as obsolete tools for achieving either personal
or social goals.[7]

Fanciful as these visions appear to those of us mired in
the unpromising present moment, they and the process
that produced them may be of signal importance in taking
us beyond the Bomb. For only if we can first imagine
ourselves past it can we in fact move past it. Lacking the
confidence that peace is in fact possible, we will never
summon the will to make it happen. Masses of people
are moved to action and self-sacrifice not by blueprints
but by visions. All too often, to our enduring regret, these
visions are skewed and self-destructive, but their appeal
and potency are undeniable. Perhaps one of the problems
has been that these visions have been the invention of a
particular individual or a party. Though they may express
themselves in the imagery of shared myth and common
identity, they have been manipulated for personal gain.
The futuring practice of Boulding and Ziegler offers ordinary people untutored in the profession and practice
of futuristic thinking an opportunity to exercise their positive imaginations in the invention of a personally shaped
destiny.

## Spinning Peace Scenarios

Whether this practice differs significantly from day-dreaming is a moot point. The adding back of a "future history" after imagining the future itself is a kind of reality check that obliges us to question our sense of the possible and the probable. In the fall of 1984, *The Christian Science Monitor* sponsored an essay contest entitled, "Peace 2010," challenging readers to take themselves forward into a moment when they are to assume peace has in some sense been attained and tell how it came about. Much to their surprise, the editors were fairly flooded with essays, receiving in all more than 1300 responses. Spinning peace scenarios is more than an exercise in fantasy, a mental sleight-of-hand. If undertaken with care and imagination, it becomes a means of clearing space, in oneself and in the world, for new and hitherto seemingly impossible things to happen. It is a means of stretching beyond one's known capabilities by overleaping self-doubts and placing oneself in the circumstances of imagined success. Confident that the feat is indeed possible, we find ourselves acting with sufficient resolution to overcome all obstacles.

This technique may have more than a little to offer us in the challenging process of inventing alternatives to the war system. The general public is not alone in wondering whether peace is actually possible. Even professional peace researchers, surveying the dismaying drift of recent events, find it difficult to muster much confidence that our proposals will be adopted any time soon. So prevalent is despair in the profession of peace work that many of us may be unaware of the degree to which we doubt the very possibilities we strive to create.

This skepticism communicates itself in a great many ways—in an over-developed capacity for critical analysis and an under-developed capacity for generating alternatives, in an over-used intellect and an under-used imagination, in a reactive rather than an initiatory politics. We tend to view peace as the poor orphaned child of war, a state of being without substance or reality in its own right, a merely hypothetical possibility. We are so certain of failure that we hobble our imaginations at the very moment when we most need to unfetter them.

> *The only means by which we can overcome the debilitating despair brought on by a sober appraisal of the odds against us is to engage in a deliberate overleaping of the obstacles between "here" and "there."*

Something more than linear and logical thinking may now be in order, something more on the order of what Edward de Bono calls "lateral thinking." The only means by which we can overcome the debilitating despair brought on by a sober appraisal of the odds against us is to engage in a deliberate overleaping of the obstacles between "here" and "there," to place ourselves in the territory of peace itself. We can then begin to survey the terrain into which we have ventured, noting what it looks like, feeling how it feels. Having premised the possibility of peace in a given circumstance, we find our minds and hearts liberated to engage in the practical consideration of how to find our way back to the present from that premised future.

This approach is not to be mistaken for wishful thinking. On the contrary, once the radical assumption has been made that peace is indeed possible, we must demonstrate an exceptional rigor in evaluating the most plausible means of reaching that state. All that we know of current trends and past history, all that we know of the personalities and predilections of the powers and peoples involved, must come into play in figuring practical means of moving between here and there. We thus simultaneously exercise those two faculties most often at odds with one another, imagination and intellect. Imagination stretches the boundaries prescribed by the intellect while the intellect disciplines the otherwise anarchic character of the imagination.

## Performing Thought Experiments

It is no small irony that this technique has thus far

found its most extensive development not in planning for peace but in planning for war. The late Herman Kahn, longtime dean of defense intellectuals, devoted his considerable intellect and curious imagination to the exploration of "unthinkable" nuclear war scenarios. He called his method "Gedanken" (thought) experiments, hypothetical inquiries into the likely consequences of undertaking various strategies in a prolonged but limited nuclear war. While we may justifiably differ with Kahn's use or abuse of intellect and imagination to test assumptions which are themselves too utterly repugnant to contemplate, we may also respect the rigor of his method and the sometimes startling objectivity of his observations.

As a means of considering policy options in the midst of a prolonged nuclear exchange, Kahn would set up a hypothetical circumstance, place his actors where he wanted them in order to evaluate the effects of his policy choice, then set the scene in motion and observe how they moved, given his knowledge of their past behavior and present tendencies. In Kahn's method, one's speculations move only forward, from a hypothetical future towards a still more distant future. But in the case of a peace scenario, one would premise a future, then work back toward the present moment. Or alternatively, premise a future, then return to the present moment and thrash one's way through the thicket of obstacles from "here" to "there."

## Blending Intellect and Imagination

Peace scenarios could become one extraordinarily useful tool in our workshop for the construction of alternatives to nuclear deterrence. They may be invented either by the individual or the group, but a group process, involving as it does the mingling of diverse perspectives, might be especially well-suited to testing the validity of scenarios. Through collective critical analysis, the group can jointly appraise what is likely to happen and what is simply not. As an integral step in the exercise, the "price of admission to the game," the group might be made responsible for providing more plausible versions of those events it did not find credible. They would thus undertake a collective invention, guiding themselves in equal measure by the faculties of intellect and imagination.

*Adding imagination to intellect gives us tangible imagery to clothe otherwise barren policy options.*

The more traditional mode of analysis and policy proposal has always been a work of the intellect. World order studies, which have projected "preferred worlds" and "relevant utopias," have been characterized by a high degree of abstraction which, despite their merit, renders them both difficult to evaluate and to penetrate. Adding imagination to intellect gives us tangible imagery to clothe otherwise barren policy options. But much more significantly, imagination adds an unpredictable and highly creative element to the mix, a lateral mode of thinking to complement the linear mode of critical policy analysis.

What I am suggesting is that we create a kind of political science fiction—that is, that we unite the three disciplines of politics, science, and the imaginative arts to evoke and evaluate the various possible routes to a sustainable peace. From politics we take a sober recognition of the primacy of self-interest and a shrewd strategy for making the highest use of that lowly motivation; from science, an objective evaluation of the risks and benefits of each choice; and from the arts, their animating quality, their capacity to evoke illuminating imagery and resonant feeling. Like science fiction, political science fiction would concern the future, but not a narrowly technical one. Unlike science fiction, it would be specifically designed as a problem-solving technique, a tool of deliberate social invention.

## Possidiction and Prefigurative Visions

In a little-known article written nearly twenty years

ago, futurist Arthur Waskow proposed a disciplined process of future imaging he called "possidiction":

It is an examination of the seriously *possible* rather than the most likely. Instead of being a prediction—that is, the author's best judgment as to what present trends are likely to produce—it is what might be called a *possidiction*—that is, the author's projection of how certain seeds of change that exist already might be made to flourish, given certain kinds of political action. The possidiction describes worlds that are, say, 30% likely—as against either worlds that are only 1% likely or those that are 60% likely. There is a serious chance they can be brought into being, but it will take a lot of doing. And the possidiction acts as an incitement to the necessary action. . . .

The whole process . . . looks like this: one develops a notion of possible social change and from that a vision of a desirable practicable future. One works out as vividly and in as much detail as possible, the way in which that practicable desirable future would work. . . . And then one works backward from that, in a kind of retroprojection, to see what kinds of change in *detail* would be necessary in order to get to that stage. In a sense this is a method of successive approximations, in which one could move from analysis of change to an image of

the future and back again, back and forth as
many times as you like, getting more and more
detailed each time.[8]

Writing more recently of a similar use of the imagination, psychotherapist Joel Kovel calls for "prefigurative
visions":

Prefiguration does not create hope, any more
than the imagination creates life. The reverse
is more nearly true: we hope, because we are
alive, and hope is an expression of our nature.
And because we hope, we sense possibilities
not given by the present but immanent in it.
Then we attempt to envisage these possibilities
prefiguratively, giving them names and
forms. . . . Prefiguration is a gesture to realize
hope. It arises from hope. Yet prefiguration has
a more active role to play. Being an act of
imagination, it creates the possibilities for
hope's realization.[9]

## Imagining More Vivid Utopias

It is in the vast literature of utopias that this practice
of envisioning is most extensively developed. The imagined worlds of past eras may well have something to tell
us about what history does to our dreams. One obser-

vation is that much of the technical invention that was prophesied has since come to pass and be surpassed, but our social inventions have more generally failed. Clearly we are more adept at technical invention, and perhaps the inert materials are less recalcitrant. But in addition, as Margaret Mead argues in a penetrating essay, our utopian imaginings tend to be "pallid" beside the scarlet traces of our dystopian fantasies.

All visions of heaven, in this world and in the next, have a curiously tasteless, pale blue and pink quality, whether the image is one of cherubim and seraphim ... or of a time when 'ploughs in peaceful industry shall supersede the sword,' when 'the dictatorship of the proletariat shall be realized in ideological completeness,' or when lions shall lie down with lambs, or of a world in which women shall have been freed from all the incidental consequences of their reproductivity and will spend long vacations with their lovers of the moment, flying Chinese kites. . . . For the past 50 years we have experimented with the compelling character of negative images, as the prophecies of the dangers of modern warfare have grown ever sharper. When warfare is upon them, men will struggle; but they sink into a kind of paralysis when there is need to fight even harder—in peacetime— to prevent the recurrence of war. We need more vivid utopias.[10]

Mead identifies three characteristics of this essential vision:
It must be vivid enough to compel the heart,
but not so vivid that one moves too quickly, by
death or emigration or the coercion of others,
to attain it; it must be so conceived that it is
sought for the sake of others rather than solely
for the self—for other men, for the whole next
generation, or for men eons ahead—with nice
adjustments which make it not too immediate
(just the next generation) and not too distant,
lest one become lost in a world without imaginable relation to the present; and it must be
complex, redundant enough to catch and hold
the imaginations of men and women of many
different types of temperament and experience, and stylized enough, in terms of culture
and period, to carry the weight of past ages of
formal esthetic molding and polishing and to
speak with cadences and lines grown powerful
by long usage.[11]

## Relevant Utopias

We must, in other words, attune our imaginations to the warp and woof of our own particular cultures and histories, even while the dream being envisioned is uni-versal. As the art of fiction attests, it is not by universalized rhetoric that most people are moved to depths of feeling but by the evocation of a particular few persons in a particular set of circumstances. We must somehow be able to imagine ourselves in their places, as less than perfect beings with our frailties still apparent but the capacity, on occasion, to transcend them. The informed imagings of alternative futurists have generally demonstrated a capacity to think large but not small, globally but not locally.

It could also be that we have been imagining worlds too perfect for the fallible creatures that we are and have thus discouraged ourselves from even making the effort to attain them. What we may be looking for is, to use the World Order Models Project's phrase in a slightly altered context, "relevant utopias," or perhaps practical utopias, comprehensive visions of an alternative society, economy and culture that retain enough of the familiar and the habitual that we can see ourselves living in them comfortably.

There are not, to my knowledge, many utopian novels being written today. Their relative scarcity, in the presence of so much literature of the nightmare, would seem to indicate that a new vogue is overdue. The arts, fiction, film and drama, may be of singular importance in attracting widespread support for social inventions that could take us beyond the Bomb, for they give a touch of warmth to otherwise cool and vaporous ideas. Dramatizing these preferred futures in all their idiosyncratic detail may give us the language and imagery that will be understood by a great many people who would otherwise never think to imagine them.

## Shifting Paradigms

In a brilliantly original essay published nearly a quarter century ago, Thomas Kuhn introduced the concept of the paradigm shift to describe the process of radical reorientation by which basic science discards one world view and adopts another. Observing the history of science, Kuhn noted that most research activity occurs in the realm of "normal science," a kind of "puzzle-solving" within a set of assumptions so deeply imbued in the culture of the age that no other perspective seems possible, let alone valid. It is only with the emergence of the "anomaly," in the form of recurring evidence which contradicts those assumptions, that "extraordinary science" is born.

"The proliferation of competing articulations, the willingness to try anything, the expression of explicit discontent, the recourse to philosophy and to debate over fundamentals, all these are symptoms of a transition from normal to extraordinary research," wrote Kuhn.[12] The character of this extraordinary science is altogether less systematic and routinized than normal science and remains a marginal occupation with little credibility among established practitioners for long epochs before a fundamental shift occurs. But when the shift finally occurs, it is often quite sudden.

*This same mode of analysis can be used to describe the shift in thinking required to take us beyond nuclear deterrence. If mutual threat and the strategy of unilateral advantage characterize our prevailing paradigm of national security, perhaps common security would best typify the perspective which must replace it.*

Although Kuhn himself did not extend his analysis from science to society (and rumor has it that he does not greatly approve the attempt), a great many other theorists have appropriated the concept to explain or characterize the shift in cultural values they see as essential to taking us beyond war and its related social crises. The concept of the paradigm shift has gained such currency in the larger peace movement no doubt in part because we have as yet no better explanation for the way fundamental assumptions change in the collective mind of a global culture. As applied to the realm of the social sciences, the concept has gone by various pairings of paradigms, from "industrial" to "trans-industrial," from "mechanistic" to "organic."

This same mode of analysis can be used to describe the shift in thinking required to take us beyond nuclear deterrence. If mutual threat and the strategy of unilateral advantage characterize our prevailing paradigm of national security, perhaps common security would best typify the perspective which must replace it. Michael Nagler applies the concept directly to the problem of war:

Emerson quite correctly said, "It was thought that built this whole portentous war establishment, and thought shall melt it away." But what he meant by "thought" is poetic shorthand for a whole way of thinking. If a true paradigm shift in science is a rare event which occurs only after a lapse of centuries, the shift we are speaking of is even rarer. It is a reorientation of the attitudes of masses of human beings not only to a particular war, not only to war in general, but to our relationships with one another. It is a step forward not only in history but in biological evolution.[13]

## The Need for Alternatives

Kuhn himself points out that no scientific world view is discarded by the culture and community it serves unless an alternative explanation is found which better conforms to present evidence. "Once it has achieved the status of a paradigm, a scientific theory is declared invalid only if

an alternative candidate is available to take its place. . . .
The decision to reject one paradigm is always simultaneously the decision to accept another."[14] This observation would seem to reinforce the arguments of Gene
Sharp, Walter Lippmann, and others that war will not be
abolished directly by disarmament but by the invention
of a number of functional substitutes which better serve
the purposes for which war currently exists—an alternative means of struggle, a "political equivalent of war,"
in Lippmann's phrase.[15]

Despite his wariness of free associations between the
social and scientific realms, Kuhn himself comments on
the parallel dynamics in political and scientific change:

Political revolutions aim to change political institutions in ways that those institutions themselves prohibit. Their success therefore
necessitates the partial relinquishment of one
set of institutions in favor of another, and in
the interim society is not fully governed by institutions at all . . . increasing numbers of individuals become estranged from political life
and behave more and more eccentrically
within it. Then, as the crisis deepens, many of
these individuals commit themselves to some
concrete proposal for the reconstruction of society in a new institutional framework.

At that point society divides into competing
camps or parties, one seeking to defend the
old institutional constellation, the others seek-

ing to institute some new one. And, once that
polarization has occurred, *political recourse
fails* (original emphasis). Because they differ
about the institutional matrix within which political change is to be achieved and evaluated,
because they acknowledge no supra-institu-
tional framework for the adjudication of revolutionary difference, the parties to a
revolutionary conflict must finally resort to the
techniques of mass persuasion, often including
force. . . . Like the choice between competing
political institutions, that between competing
paradigms proves to be a choice between in-
compatible modes of community life.[16]

## The Perennial Vision

But it is to Fred Polak, the father of alternative futurism, that we must turn for a final view of his perspective
on the question we have set for ourselves:

Although much of our thinking about the future today is inevitably in terms of choosing
between the two competing images of the future which the East and the West have set before us, we must in the long run pass beyond
these dichotomies which paint the future in
black and white. Neither Russia nor America

alone can spawn the future. The image of the future, at its best, has always been universal in character, a vision to serve and foster the growth of all mankind.

At a time when the lack of such a vision seems to be driving us to self-destruction, it is well to remember that one of the most potent and enduring visions in the history of man has been that of a Thousand Years' Reign of Peace. This is a vision which is never entirely absent from the hearts of men and women who come together to bear children and build a home. If the man leaves home and wife and child to go forth to war, as he has so often done in the past, it is only that he may in the end return and continue building in peace. If the woman endures hardship bravely and finds ways to survive when there seems to be no hope of survival, it is only that the child of her womb may live to build a better world.

The sparks of this universal vision lie in every human spirit in every land. A vision of the future which falls short of this universality will in the end leave the earth a smoking ruin. The same tool cannot serve simultaneously as sword and ploughshare, and the scope of the vision will determine the final use to which the tool is put.[17]

# CONCLUSION:
## Are There Better Games than War?

> *"If optimism and pessimism have be-*
> *come increasingly irrelevant in our ter-*
> *rible dilemma, there is great reason*
> *nonetheless to practice the ancient vir-*
> *tue of hope.... Poor as the present out-*
> *look for peace is, we can take refuge in*
> *the realization, coming more and more*
> *to be accepted, that nothing except our-*
> *selves prevents us from consigning wars*
> *to the unhappy past. They correspond*
> *neither to God's will nor to the dictates*
> *of necessity."*[1]
>
> — J. GLENN GRAY

Having turned not a few stones in the search for a world
beyond the Bomb, we have come up with what some
might call scattered debris—the wrong kind of "beyond"—but which I would rather choose to call the foundation rocks on which to build a more stable global
community. What I see in the somewhat miscellaneous
evidence compiled here is an implicit consensus of perspectives amid a variety of approaches. Being still too

close to the material to discern, I can't tell whether this apparent congruence results from my own selectivity or from a spontaneous and unrecognized measure of agreement among alternative theorists themselves. Certainly one could produce a host of other thinkers who would disagree with nearly all the values and assumptions of this group. And it might be worthwhile to challenge ourselves by considering a few genuinely contrary perspectives, since before any such ideas will float in the mainstream of political discourse, they will need to prove their buoyancy against all manner of deflationary criticism.

> *Insofar as we do disagree, why not let our hundred flowers bloom?*

But it seems to me that our first task is to locate the common ground in alternative thinking and to enlarge its domain wherever that can be done without violence to the integrity of personal visions and values. Although perspectives in the alternative movement are by no means identical, they are often complementary and seldom mutually exclusive. It may sometimes be pride rather than principle that keeps us from agreeing with one another. And insofar as we do disagree, why not let our hundred flowers bloom? One of the richest traditions in alternative thinking is that it is not an ideology—at least, not yet—and we can be thankful for that. The point

of using the term, "alternative," is to encourage inno-
vative thinking of every variety without judging it against
an arbitrary doctrinal line. When there are too few options on the table and too few in the public mind, it is
our first order of business to propagate new choices, to
initiate a season of invention.

I use the term, "invention," advisedly. But I am not at
all certain that structures and processes can be invented
in the social and political realms as readily as they are
invented in the technical and technological. We know
very little as yet about how ideas seed themselves and
grow, how nations and peoples change their minds about
the world. My hunch is that it is not a highly rational
process but a deeply emotional and largely subconscious
response, a reaction more to events than to ideas. For
this reason I am skeptical that our political solutions and
social inventions, elegant as they may be, will of themselves persuade sufficient numbers of people to adopt a
new way of thinking and acting. We will need somehow
to harness events and trends already present in the culture in order to gain sufficient momentum for a transformation.

## Legitimizing Peace

Such change as is possible will likely continue to resist
being confined within our best-laid plans but will be improvised from a hybrid of chance and necessity. "Mud-

dling through," it might be called, this patchwork process of mending human history. But to say that ideas do not govern history is not to say that they are without effect. Without the insistence of many minds for many years upon the idea of freedom as an inalienable human right, slavery would still be seen as legitimate. Would a similar insistence upon the idea of peace and the illegitimacy of the Bomb have a similar effect?

Throughout this report I have used the term, "the Bomb," as shorthand for the cluster of perils surrounding nuclear weapons. But in the course of my research and thinking I have found my own definitions blurring. I have found these weapons to be so integral to the war system, so central to its functioning, and so fully expressive of its ethos, that I can no longer separate the problem of the Bomb from the problem of war. Are nuclear weapons the disease itself or simply its most egregious symptom? If we focus too narrowly on nuclear technology as the primal source rather than the prime symptom of the war disease, might we not well be inviting a technological end run to achieve the same destructiveness by other means?

Again it is George Kennan who best expresses for me the inseparability of the twin problems of nuclear weapons and war:

I am now bound to say that while the earliest possible elimination of nuclear weaponry is of no less vital importance in my eyes than it ever was, this would not be enough, in itself, to

give Western civilization even an adequate
chance of survival. War itself, as a means of
settling differences at least among the great industrial powers, will have to be in some way
ruled out; and with it there will have to be dismantled (for without this the whole outlawing
of war would be futile) the greater part of the
vast military establishments now maintained
with a view to the possibility that war might
take place. . . .
    No one could be more aware than I am of
the difficulty of ruling out war among great
states. It is not possible to write any sure pre-
scription as to how this might be achieved,
particularly because the course of international
life is not, and cannot be, determined over the
long term by specific treaties or charters
agreed upon at a single moment in history and
reflecting only the outlooks and circumstances
of that particular moment. It is the ingrained
habits and assumptions of men, and above all
of men in government, which alone can guarantee any enduring state of peaceful relations
among men.[2]

    Moving beyond war, at least among the great powers,
is a still more daunting objective than moving beyond
nuclear weapons. There are many who would say that
moving beyond war is not a program but a Christmas
wish. And they would be half right. But it may be equally

unrealistic to assume that war among nations with nuclear weapons can reliably be kept free of their use. The Bomb's sole great contribution to the cause of peace has been its tendency to render war of any kind less thinkable. But nuclear deterrence, like the radioactivity within the weapons themselves, is a decaying substance whose half-life may well be shorter than we think. It is not and cannot become the basis for a stable peace.

> *What we need is a many-faceted substitute for the manifold functions that war has traditionally served.*

If war is somehow to be ruled out, the feat will not be accomplished by treaty alone. It will be achieved in part by the deliberate invention of new arenas and instruments for the resolution and management of conflict, but also by a highly improvised process of unconscious cultural adaptation to the imperative of survival. What we need, as Walter Lippmann suggests, is a "political equivalent for war"; or, as William James suggests, a "moral equivalent"; or, as Gene Sharp suggests, an alternative means of struggle. What we need is a many-faceted substitute for the manifold functions that war has traditionally served, a replacement set of institutions, attitudes, rituals, habits and myths that better serve the preservation of the species.

"Is there a better game than war?" asks Robert Fuller. "[This is] meant to be a provocative question, suggesting that war has in fact been an activity that men and women have played and have loved. They have also hated it, but it's crucial if we're ever going to bypass or transcend war-making that we admit our own eternal fascination with the business of it, with the fact that it provides moments of individual exhilaration, camaraderie, nobility, leadership, courage and glory that other human activities seldom match. The horrible side of war is well-known and usually focused on, but until we acknowledge our secret attraction to it we're likely to keep on 'doing' it. . . .

"War is a collective activity and as such has been a provider of myths—unifying overviews of triumph and tragedy in which each individual has a role. If another game can in fact be substituted for war, it will have to meet not only the individual's need for challenge and adventure, but also the collective need for an integrative myth that renders life and lives meaningful."[3]

Beyond the Bomb and beyond war is peace itself, about which we know so very little. When I began this inquiry, I commented to a colleague familiar with the territory that I felt as if we were standing on the frontier of the Thirteen Colonies in the year 1750, gazing west and wondering what lay beyond. "You're an optimist," he said. "I would sooner say we're standing in medieval Europe, looking west towards a New World no one has yet seen." However it may be, the journey into this last virgin territory is a heroic quest fully worthy of the warrior's mantle. And of our own most spirited engagement.

# EPILOGUE:
## The Bomb Has Already Fallen

> *"Do not go gentle into that good night.*
> *Rage, rage against the dying of the*
> *light."*[1]
>
> – DYLAN THOMAS

The effort to endure a perpetual condition of abstract terror has wrought subtly profound changes in the psyches of those living in this first generation since the birth of the Bomb. In what ways has the presence of nuclear weapons changed our hearts and minds? There is a growing literature that seeks to describe and analyze these effects.

Statistical surveys reveal a profoundly contradictory relationship between Americans and their nuclear weapons, and a deep confusion about the actual thrust of current governmental policy. A recent survey conducted by the Public Agenda Foundation and Brown University's Center for Foreign Policy Development traces a remarkable shift in public attitudes toward the Bomb in

the years since its invention. In 1949, 59% of those surveyed believed it was "a good thing that the atomic bomb
was developed. . . . The atomic bomb, for all its power,
was not viewed as a reprehensible weapon or something
that might, one day, be used against us. . . . By 1982,
however . . . the Gallup survey revealed that Americans'
thinking had undergone a radical change: now nearly two
in three Americans (65%) had come to believe that the
development of the bomb was a 'bad thing.'"

While twenty-nine years ago only a quarter of the public (27%) believed that "mankind would be destroyed in
an all-out atomic or hydrogen bomb war," by 1984 an
overwhelming 89% believed that there could be no win-
ners in such a war and that both sides would be destroyed.
Most startling of all is the public's perceptions of the
future: 75% of women and 78% of persons under thirty
believe that "if we and the Soviets keep building missiles
instead of negotiating to get rid of them, it's only a matter
of time before they are used . . . Nearly 40%—and half
of those under thirty—say that all-out nuclear war is
likely within the next ten years."[2] At the same time a
sizeable minority believes that "the U.S. should lead the
world out of the nuclear arms race by unilaterally reducing our stockpile of nuclear weapons" (43%), while
33% believe that "by 1990 it should be U.S. policy *never*
to use nuclear weapons."[3]

# A Divergence between Experts and Laymen

Perhaps most significant in the Public Agenda study is the apparent division between expert and citizen opinion concerning nuclear weapons policy. While a great majority of the public appears to believe that the United States possesses nuclear weapons for the sole purpose of deterring a direct attack on its own territory, many nuclear strategists appear to accept without qualms a broad range of supplementary functions for these instruments. Furthermore, "almost unanimously, the experts regard as unrealistic the sense of imminent nuclear war found in large segments of the public . . . Though most regard the present reliance on nuclear deterrence as uncomfortable from a security point of view, and some find it a morally repugnant way to preserve peace, the majority of experts sees no alternative to some form of deterrence based on nuclear weapons, at least for the immediate future. The public consensus is less accepting of continuing dependence on nuclear weapons."[4]

The divergence between expert and lay opinion becomes most obvious in the growing skepticism with which lay citizens appear to view expert opinion on matters of war and peace. In what may be the most telling and hopeful finding in the study, citizens reject by overwhelming margins (77% to 21%) the premise fostered by many experts that "the subject of nuclear weapons is too complex for people like me to think about; that should be left to the President and the experts."[5] Jerome Wiesner, himself a pre-eminent expert (former science adviser to President Kennedy and former president of MIT), stresses the importance of disenthralling ourselves of the notion that the experts know better.

It is often suggested that secret information exists that would argue against a nuclear freeze or a test ban or some other logical arms-limitation measure. But there are no secrets on the vital issues that determine the course of the arms race. Each citizen should realize that on such critical issues as what constitutes a deterrent and how many nuclear weapons are enough his or her judgments are as good as those of a president or secretary of defense, perhaps even better since the layperson is not subject to all of the confusing pressures that influence people in official positions. It is important for citizens to realize that their government has no monopoly on wisdom or special knowledge . . .[6]

## Losing Faith in the Future

Studies like the Public Agenda report reveal much about conscious public opinion regarding the Bomb, but

they leave largely concealed the less quantifiable subter-
ranean emotions we harbor, feelings far removed from
policy formulae and often so deeply buried that we are
not always aware of their presence. There is a modest
and growing literature of cultural critique which seeks
to probe the psychological and sociological effects of living in the shadow of the Bomb. Basing its conclusions not
primarily on data but on speculation informed by a knowledge of psychology, sociology, history, anthropology, and
related fields (and sometimes tested by in-depth interviews), this work does not pretend to be scientifically
precise but remains powerfully suggestive of the deeper
truths which bind us to the Bomb and which, if acknowledged, might free us from its spell.

Perhaps best known and most extensive is the work of
Robert Jay Lifton, whose prior experience with Hiroshima survivors led him to consider the manifold impacts
of the Bomb on the individual conscience. Lifton asserts
that in response to the threat of extinction, most citizens
have suppressed their latent terror in distraction and denial, resulting in the acute loss of sensitivity to other aspects
of life he calls "psychic numbing." But this loss extends
well beyond the present moment. In Lifton's view, the
specter of the Bomb severs the individual's sense of con-
tinuity with both past and future:

From the standpoint of psychic impact, it does
not matter much whether we imagine the end
of *all* or merely *most* human life. Either way,
we can no longer feel certain of biological pos-

terity. We are in doubt about the future of *any* group—of one's family, geographical or ethnic confreres, people, or nation. The image is that of human history and human culture simply terminating. The idea of *any* human future becomes a matter of profound doubt. In that image we or perhaps our children are the last human beings. There is no one after us to leave anything to. We become cut off, collectively self-enclosed, something on the order of a vast remnant.[7]

Children, of course, are most vulnerable to whatever psychic fallout there may be from the bomb that has not yet exploded. Much study has been done these past few years of the effects of the arms race on the hearts and minds of U.S. and Soviet children. Drs. John Mack, William Beardslee, and Eric Chivian of Harvard Medical School have conducted extensive interviews among schoolchildren in both the United States and Soviet Union. *In the Nuclear Shadow: What Can the Children Tell Us?*, an affecting film by Vivian Verdon-Roe, records the feelings of schoolchildren in Northern California about the Bomb and their future.[8] The Nuclear Ecology Research Project, which also studies the emotional effects of the Bomb on U.S. and Soviet children, reports that "we are facing a mental health problem of epidemic proportions."[9]

All of these researchers report that children do not have to be asked to think about the Bomb: they have already thought about it and have reached their own conclusions. We may recall the startling finding of the Public Agenda survey that fully half those under 30 years old believe nuclear war is likely in the next ten years. Dr. Chivian reports that while both sets of superpower children recognize the imminence of danger, the Americans are actually somewhat more resigned to helplessness and the inevitability of events, while Soviet children appear to place faith (undue, perhaps) in those in authority to protect them from harm.

But not all psychologists agree that children are being greatly affected by living with the Bomb. Some believe the symptoms of unease found in many children today may be equally attributable to any of a number of other perils of living in the modern age—television, cars, street violence, divorce, and other apparently disintegrative trends and phenomena. Child psychologist Robert Coles, whose interviews with poor black and white children in the rural South during the Sixties discovered in them an extraordinary suffering and wisdom, has argued most forcefully that the notion of "psychic numbing" is a class judgment by the self-righteous and the affluent. By asserting that others are not responding to the threat of nuclear war because they are too numbed to feel it, Coles argues, those with few material problems ask those with a great many of them to care about a threat so distant they can neither see nor sense it, while a half-dozen more intimate and inescapable threats besiege them. Thus we may not be able to understand why others appear numbed to the nuclear threat until we become aware of our own numbness to their more immediate sources of anguish.

## Nuclearism: The Religion of Hard Technology

These are personal effects, occurring within the hearts and minds of individuals. But there is also a level of social effects, trends in popular culture supporting and opposing the Bomb as well as societal processes affected by its presence. Here we have least recourse to actual data and must content ourselves for the moment with informed speculation, granting that these are hypotheses and conjectures still to be proven, and perhaps unprovable. Lewis Mumford has long viewed nuclear weapons as a symptom and expression of a larger cultural movement, the heedless pursuit of "technics" and power in defiance of nature and all limits.[10] Others have examined the artifacts of contemporary youth culture and have found among them a growing obsession, even a fascination, with the imagery of post-apocalypse. Paul Brians has studied portrayals of nuclear holocaust in fiction and film. He concludes:

Not since the euphoria that swept the nation after the bombing of Hiroshima and Nagasaki nearly 40 years ago have images of nuclear war been so widespread in popular culture. Americans, it seems, are learning to love the nuclear bomb—especially youngsters, who are escaping their anxiety by embracing the bomb as an adventure . . . This trend signals the end of an era in which awed respect was granted the prospect of atomic annihilation . . . What is new is the bravado with which books and films depict the prospect of Armageddon. What was shocking black comedy in the movie "Dr. Strangelove" is now the norm for many young people. Some of this is adolescent posturing—the equivalent of flaunting swastikas, to alienate adults—but much of it, I suspect, reflects the despair about the future that turns up in surveys of youths' opinion about nuclear war. Video games, films, music and books are reconciling a generation to nuclear war as inevitable.[11]

Other observers have described what they see as a kind of social myth bound up with the Bomb—a nuclear ideology that has generated over the years the hallowed ritual, arcane language, secretive mystery, and encompassing culture appropriate to a new technological religion. Nuclearism, Robert Jay Lifton calls this latter-day faith, "a search for grace and glory in which technical-scientific transcendence, apocalyptic destruction, national power, personal salvation, and committed individual identity all become psychically bound up with the bomb."[12]

"The bomb became surrounded with its own ideology,"

writes sociologist Alan Wolfe about the early years of the nuclear age, "a set of meanings that enable the American people to reconcile themselves to their nuclear reality— a folk culture of nuclear weapons. According to this ideology, the bomb could be used only for Good because the society that developed it represented the Good. . . .

> *America deserved the bomb because America was unique, and the proof of America's uniqueness was that it had developed the bomb.*

The bomb, the most destructive instrument ever created to advance the aims of war, would guarantee that the world would never again have to go to war. This democratic folk culture that legitimated the bomb evolved into a completely self-enclosed worldview: America deserved the bomb because America was unique, and the proof of America's uniqueness was that it had developed the bomb."[13] The Soviet Union, of course, views its nuclear weapons in much the same moral terms, calling its own arsenal a "peace bomb" maintained solely to deter the American "war bomb."

While the Public Agenda survey indicates that Americans have been growing gradually disaffected with the Bomb over the years since its invention, several significant groups spanning the social spectrum appear to remain wedded to the nuclear faith. The engineers and technicians, politicians and publicists of the nuclear establishment together constitute what some observers have called a self-appointed "nuclear clergy" guarding the secrecy and sanctity of the Bomb. Theirs is generally a sophisticated and secularized belief structure, notable for its well-groomed appearance of rationality and objectivity. Despite mounting evidence of its deleterious effects, they remain exponents of "hard tech," the technologies of centralized power, resource exploitation, and unbounded destructiveness. As public attitudes have gradually shifted away from uncritical acceptance of nuclear weapons and energy, supporters of the Bomb have restyled their rhetoric to include the now obligatory expressions of abhorrence, but most remain loyal to the faith. Nuclear weapons are a manifest evil, they argue, but a necessary evil so long as the other side has them.

## Attractions to Apocalypse

Beside the apparent rationality of nuclear strategists and technicians a much vaster non-rational phenomenon has grown up in recent years, an ostensibly religious movement whose televised prophets embrace nuclear weapons as their ultimate protectors. "Nuclear fundamentalism," as Wolfe and Lifton call it, is a blend of religious zealotry, xenophobia, uncritical faith in high technology, and nuclear warfighting doctrine which so shrouds the consequences of nuclear catastrophe in the mantle of inevitability and righteousness that believers are positively drawn to yearn for its occurrence. This attraction to apocalypse is most widely seen among the televised evangelical ministries of the New Right, where it is often bound up with scarcely concealed motives of commercial plunder. "Become an End-Time Partner by sending a generous contribution towards the launching of this End-Time Prophetic Ministry... THE END IS NEAR," states a flyer distributed by mail to many U.S. households in 1983.[14]

We might wish to believe that this primitivism of emotion and belief is confined to those without access to power. But the appetite for salvation by extermination is equally and far more menacingly present among the highest priests of the order. "I have read the Book of Revelation and, yes, I believe the world is going to end— by an act of God, I hope—but every day I think that time is running out," declares U.S. Defense Secretary Caspar Weinberger, while President Reagan himself confides to the Reverend Falwell, "Jerry, I sometimes believe we're heading for Armageddon very fast right now."[15]

## Biblical Themes

This marriage of faith and terror, salvation and apocalypse, has long been characteristic of evangelical Christianity. But now it appears in the service of the technocratic state as a justification for ultimate concentrations of power. Psychoanalyst Joel Kovel argues that it is not the renegade, acting alone or in tight conspiracy, who most effectively manipulates the instruments of terror, but the state itself.[16] With a vastly greater diversity of technical and mental weaponry at its disposal the state can manage terror so as to cause its subjects to cling to it in fright as to a protecting god. In the ultimate inversion of imagery, the Bomb itself becomes a kind of deity. It is a blend of Old and New Testament themes: revenge, destruction, and salvation of the elect, all by grace of the Bomb.

The sources of this attraction to extinction may run very deep indeed. The extent to which human beings "wish" death upon themselves has long been a matter of extraordinary controversy among psychologists and philosophers. The case will likely never be settled, nor need it be for us to move beyond the Bomb. But it may be important to acknowledge that within some of us may reside a certain attraction the very thought of which our civilized minds find repugnant. It may well be that in denying death, or more rightly, in denying our *fear* of death, we are driven to perform those very acts which bring death closer to us.

This attraction may not be altogether perverse in origin. But it may become so when its expression in meaningful ritual is denied. "The condition that is attractive should not ... be necessarily equated with biological death," writes Steven Kull, a psychologist who has examined the relation between nuclear weapons and what he calls "the desire for world destruction." " . . . The desire for self-destruction may not be an actual desire for death but rather for *a transformation of experience* [original emphasis]. It may be that when one's experience lacks the desired quality of unity, a level of frustration is reached in which there is a willingness to undergo the painful processes necessary to alter one's state radically."[17] Thus the impulse to apocalypse in nuclear fundamentalism may not be so much a death wish as a fantasy of selective salvation, a yearning to be released, in a sudden, searing flash of light, from all the limitations and frustrations of ordinary life, to be reborn free of restraints into an environment scoured of all hostile or competing forces.

## Toward a "Final Solution"

But fundamentalism is not the only form of expression for such sentiments. Far more sophisticated minds have found themselves attracted to this latter-day "final solution," hoping to relieve an otherwise unbearable tension of uncertainty by means of an event of sudden and irrevocable finality. With brilliant irony, Alia Johnson captures the flavor of the feeling:

> it would be so exciting
> it would be so powerful
> it would punish us for our sins

things wouldn't be so boring anymore
we could get back to basics
we would remember who we love
it would be so loud
it would be so hot
the mushroom clouds would rise up
we could start over
we wouldn't have to be afraid of it anymore
we wouldn't have to be afraid anymore
we would finally have done it
better than Raskolnikov
it would release our anger
in the ultimate tantrum
then we could rest[18]

## Imagining the Absolute Enemy

Whatever the nature of these self-destructive emotional tendencies—be they suicidal, omnicidal, or simply escapist—they are not, I think, so central a motive force in support of the nuclear state as is the ancient and perennial fear of the enemy, a fear masterfully orchestrated by politicians and publicists in both superpowers. "Once a nation bases its security on an absolute weapon, such as the atom bomb," writes Patrick Blackett, "it becomes psychologically necessary to believe in an absolute enemy."[19] A quarter century ago, social psychologist Urie Bronfenbrenner recognized a phenomenon of "mirror imaging" in the enemy archetypes evoked by both superpowers.[20] It is the familiar psychological process of projection, writes Jerome Frank, a deft shifting of the truth by which "opponents attribute the same virtues to themselves and the same vices to each other."[21] Findings in the field of attribution theory indicate that enemy images are sustained by a disposition to accept as truth only those facts or assertions that meet our preconceived beliefs. Thus we tend to believe only the worst of our enemies and the best of ourselves.

There is at the heart of nuclear deterrence an impulse that leads both sides to reach for effect, a felt need to exaggerate the nature of the threat and the justifiable response. President Nixon is reported to have sought to make Ho Chi Minh think him "a bit crazy"—crazy enough, at least, to have him believe Nixon would dare to use nuclear weapons on North Vietnam. It is in the nature of nuclear strategy as now practiced that threats must be ceaselessly renewed—and indeed, enlarged—or their deterrent effect fades. Inflation of threats thus grows still more costly to the national treasury than inflation of currency.

## Relations of Rivals

These threat cycles contribute to a self-driven and perpetually escalating rivalry, a competition whose psychology bears comparison to rival relations on many other levels of human interaction. The psychological causes and effects of rivalry have received scant attention in the literature but they may well figure as largely in arms races and wars as do the strategic and political considerations we conventionally assume to be the primary determinants of policy. For despite their most vehement protestations to the contrary, rivals share an intimate relation, bound close as brothers by their mutual hostility. In motives, goals, and means, the superpowers are perhaps more alike than different. It is not in fact their differences that gall them but their unacknowledged similarities. Each faults in the other what each cannot see or accept in itself. Yet the vehemence with which each condemns the motives of the other hints strongly that both harbor similar intentions.

The relation between rivals is in fact so intimate that they may be seen to create one another as enemies, selecting their sparring partners by a paradoxical process of negative infatuation. In denying respect to one another, rivals build and brandish weapons of great psychological potency. Yet ironically this denial yokes them more tightly than any treaty of alliance, since each demands respect from the one least inclined to render it. Each has something the other seeks and can find nowhere else. Each claims all truth for itself and denies all truth to the other. Yet taken on balance, it likely belongs in part to both. Rivals are would-be teachers of one another, each lacking the patience and will to learn the essential truths the other has to offer.

# Playing Helpless: The Psychology of the Victim

But where in all this stands the ordinary citizen, the "innocent civilian" that Freeman Dyson calls the "victim"? The majority has tried mightily, but with only mixed success, to forget altogether that the menace exists. Consigning the Bomb's fate to the status of a natural event wholly beyond human intervention (like an earthquake or a volcanic eruption) or to a conspiracy among a privileged elite equally beyond accountability, most ordinary citizens have come to view the arms race as a kind of perpetual motion machine, set in operation a generation ago and assumed to proceed as it has into the indefinite future. Unless, of course . . . A race, in short, without a finish line.

Most citizens in both nuclear and non-nuclear states have thus neither embraced nor rejected the Bomb but have sought an uneasy coexistence, wishing it weren't there but doing little to make it so. For a brief period during the early Eighties, large numbers of Americans appeared to be awakening from this self-induced slumber, registering large majorities in national polls favoring a nuclear freeze. But when thwarted by a cleverly intransigent President, a compliant Senate, and media distracted by trivia, many lapsed back into resignation. The "second numbing" which has since followed appears to be more conscious than the first, a willful suppression of alarm in the face of facts nearly everyone now knows, a deliberate decision to forget about what many imagine cannot be changed.

> *Is it possible that groups and cultures as a whole also become unconsciously self-hurting and available to be victims?*

It has long been the habit of civilians in the nuclear generation to believe we are helpless victims of forces beyond our control. But the truth may be more ambiguous. Recent studies of the psychology of victims indicate that victims sometimes unwittingly conspire in their own destruction. Identifying with the aggressor (the nuclear state, the Bomb itself) as their only apparent source of strength when they feel themselves to be intolerably weak, victims sometimes place themselves in situations and relationships which on some level they know will hurt them.

"Victims and oppressors give themselves to one another, fuse with one another, and exploit one another—anything not to be alone with their own life and death," writes Israel Charny, who has extensively studied the psychology of genocide. "Is it possible that groups and cultures as a whole also become unconsciously self-hurting and available to be victims? If we come to understand the self-hurting of individuals as a way of trying to reduce terrible fears rather than as a direct effort to get hurt, can we also think of groups of people [as] trying to flee life's risks together?"[22]

## Our Own Executioners

"Psychologists recognize two kinds of helplessness," writes Nicholas Humphrey:

*Learned* helplessness may develop when, for example, a person has repeatedly found that previous efforts to take control of his own life have genuinely come to nothing; he loses all faith in his own effectiveness and carries over to the present a picture of himself as someone unable any longer to influence events. But there is also a different sort of helplessness: a *superstitious* helplessness where a person's belief in his own impotence has no basis in experience, but results instead from nothing more than a superstitious premonition that his life, and perhaps the life of the whole world, is set on an unalterable course—unalterable, that is, by human agency . . .

Superstitious helplessness can take the fight out of a man quite as effectively as any more reasonable fear. Cordelia Edvardson, one of the delegates to the 1981 reunion of Holocaust

survivors, described how some of the Jews in
Germany fell victim to just such a paralysing
superstition. "Of course," she says, "we wanted
to survive, but we were not at all sure we had
the right to survive." And when a person no
longer believes he has the right to survive, his
helplessness itself is killing.[23]

In the case of the nuclear threat, of course, we are not
victims alone but in part our own executioners. Whose
hands, after all, assemble the missile components? Whose
dollars pay the taxes that finance research? Who pours
the concrete for the silos? Why do we sentence ourselves
to death and commission our own coffins? Perhaps because we dread still more than our known terrors the
unknown terrors we might incite by resisting our fate.
These risks are tangible and not to be lightly dismissed.
Those who resisted in the Warsaw Ghetto while others
sleepwalked into the ovens endured the agonies of pro-
tracted struggle against an unremitting and merciless aggressor they knew they could not overcome—and most
died. Was it worth the effort to resist? Those who survived
would likely answer yes.

## The Strategies of Self-Rescue

But how do we cease being victims of our most malig-
nant invention, the Bomb? How do we break out of the

victim's self-willed fate? We may need to begin by acknowledging that in a psychic sense the Bomb has already fallen. We are survivors of an emotional holocaust of incalculable dimensions. "The nuclear winter is already here," writes psychiatrist John Mack. "It is a cold winter of the soul."[24] Therapist Joanna Macy asserts that many Americans (and others as well) are afflicted by a sense of impotence and despair in their responses to the manifold and unprecedented threats now facing the planet. The anxiety and anguish inflicted by the loss of a dependable future remain largely unconscious and unexpressed in most people, but nevertheless profoundly affect their attitudes and behavior.

Over the past several years, Macy and a host of others in an international network called Interhelp[25] have evolved a method for dealing with despair in the nuclear age. Recognizing that it is not healthy to grieve alone, they have devised a format in which small groups are encouraged to explore and express their feelings about the state of the world in an atmosphere of mutual support. Despair work provides a safe haven in which to release emotions previously held secret even from one's own conscious mind—in community with others. Thus the process itself helps reforge the bonds of trust sundered in part by the atomizing effects of the detonation of the Bomb inside our collective awareness.

Insofar as we deny our concern, we continue to be victims of a fate we decline to change. But beneath the feigned indifference, suppressed by our premature burial of the will to endure, is alarm. Beneath the too quick resignation is resistance and perhaps renaissance, the will and strength to prevail. In the space that opens when we let ourselves care what happens to the world, energies emerge that we had not known were there, capacities to transform ourselves and perhaps the world. Discovering we need not be victims, we become actors in our own right, volunteers on a mission of self-rescue.

## Seeking the Sources of Peace

But this discovery is not an end in itself. And indeed, in the absence of a more attractive endpoint, few will be drawn to endure the gauntlet of painful feelings occasioned by admitting one's concern. To move beyond the Bomb, we will need not only, as Einstein said, a substantially new way of thinking, but a substantially new way of feeling, about both ourselves and our world. And it is here where existing resources fail us. For though there is a small corpus of work on the psychology of war—its cultural and emotional roots, its non-rational sources— virtually nothing has been written about the psychology of peace. By the phrase, psychology of peace, I refer to those attitudes and emotions which foster peace at both individual and social levels and the ways in which they are nurtured. We have done some thinking, though not nearly enough, about the roots of war. But we have not yet asked in any speculative detail what are the non-political sources of peace, the cultural and emotional conditions in which peace can take root and thrive.

Nor should we limit our focus to the purely personal. As social enterprises, war and the war system generate a characteristic culture and communal myth. We live in an increasingly militarized global culture in which weapons are ultimate icons of power and the Bomb is the reigning deity. Can we imagine and evoke a culture of peace in which the preservation of life in its natural splendor and diversity instead becomes the highest good? And more importantly, can we create a culture and myth sufficiently compelling and attractive to overcome the species' lingering but obsolescent fascination with war?

These are not idle questions to be set aside until more practical matters have been settled. For even after we have determined the wisest policies and strategies to pursue, we still require the will to make peace which only changes of heart and mind can supply. Where there is a will, there may well be a way, but where that will is weak, the better ways may never matter.

## Alternative Defense: Protection without Threat

1. The European Security Study, *Strengthening Conventional Deterrence in Europe* (New York: St. Martins, 1983).

2. The Alternative Defence Commission, *Defence Without the Bomb* (London: Taylor and Francis, 1983).

3. Alexander Macleod, "Britain's Labour Party Spells Out Its Non-Nuclear Defense Plan," *Christian Science Monitor* (July 30, 1984) p. 27.

4. Frank Barnaby and Egbert Boeker, *Defence Without Offence: Non-Nuclear Defence for Europe* (London: Housmans, 1983), p. 58.

5. The Boston Study Group, *Winding Down: The Price of Defense* (San Francisco: W.H. Freeman, 1982), p. 11.

6. Harold Feiveson and Fran von Hippel, "Minimal Deterrence" (Preliminary outline of a book, 3 March 1984), p. 1.

7. Randall Forsberg, "Confining the Military to Defense as a Route to Disarmament" *World Policy Journal* (Winter, 1984).

8. Jonathan Schell, "The Abolition," *The New Yorker* (January 9, 1984).

9. Freeman Dyson, *Disturbing the Universe* (New York: Harper and Row, 1979); and *Weapons and Hope* (New York: Harper and Row, 1984).

10. Dyson, *Weapons and Hope,* p. 277.

11. Ibid., p. 293.

12. Ibid., p. 290.

13. The term, "transarmament," has been used in differing contexts by different scholars to describe a shift either from offensive to defensive weapons and strategies (Fischer and Galtung) or from armed force of any kind to civilian-based defense (Gene Sharp). The term apparently originates with Kenneth Boulding in the 1930's and was reintroduced by Theodor Ebert, the West German nonviolent defense theorist, in the 1960's. As used by Ebert, it referred to wholly non-military defense. The confusion is a symptom, perhaps, of the lamentable lack of contact among peace researchers.

14. Dietrich Fischer, *Preventing War in the Nuclear Age* (Totowa, New Jersey: Rowman and Allanheld, 1984), p. 108.

15. Ibid., p. 113.

**Alternative Security:** Not by Arms Alone

1. Robert C. Johansen, *Toward an Alternative Security System: Moving Beyond the Balance of Power in the Search for World Security* World Policy Paper #24 (New York: World Policy Institute, 1983), pp. 28-30.

2. Johan Galtung, *There Are Alternatives: Four Roads to Peace and Security* (Nottingham: Spokesman, 1984), p. 192.

3. Daniel Deudney, *Whole Earth Security: Towards a Geopolitics of Peace*, Worldwatch Paper 55 (July, 1983), pp. 20-21.

4. Ibid., p. 41.

5. Earl Ravenal, *Defining Defense: The 1985 Military Budget* (Washington: The Cato Institute, 1984), p. 42.

6. Ibid., pp. 36-37.

7. Ibid., pp. 5, 14.

8. *The Security Project: The First Report* (New York: World Policy Institute, June, 1984), p. 23.

9. Ibid., p. 33.

**World Order:** As if People Mattered

1. Quoted by Stanley Hoffman in, "Report of the Conference on Conditions of World Order—June 12-19, 1965, Villa Serbelloni, Bellagio, Italy," *Daedalus* (Spring, 1965), p. 456.

2. Richard Falk, "Contending Approaches to World Order," in Gordon Feller, et al, *Peace and World Order Studies: A Curriculum Guide*, 3d ed. (New York: Institute for World Order, 1981), pp. 41, 43.

3. Johan Galtung, "A Structural Theory of Imperialism," *Journal of Peace Research* 8 (1971), pp. 81-111.

4. Robert C. Johansen, *The National Interest and the Human Interest: An Analysis of U.S. Foreign Policy* (Princeton: Princeton University Press, 1980).

5. Falk, "Contending Approaches to World Order," in Feller, op. cit., p. 49.

6. Ibid., p. 48.

7. Richard Falk, "Normative Initiatives and Demilitarization: A Third System Approach," in Richard Falk, Samuel Kim, Saul Mendlovitz, *Toward a Just World Order* (Boulder: Westview, 1982).

8. Announcement, *Commission for a Just World Peace* (November 8, 1983), p. 9.

9. Patrician and Gerald Mische, *Toward a Human World Order* (New York: Paulist Press, 1977), p. 272.

---

**Disarmament:** The Road Not Taken

1. Grenville Clark and Louis Sohn, *World Peace Through World Law* (Cambridge: Harvard University Press, 1958), p. xvi.

2. Marcus Raskin, *A Program Treaty for Security and General Disarmament* (Washington: Institute for Policy Studies, 1984), p. 13.

3. Ibid., p. 5.

4. Randall Forsberg, "Confining the Military to Defense as a Route to Disarmament," *World Policy Journal* (Winter, 1984), p. 288.

5. Ibid., p. 287.

6. Ibid., p. 310.

7. See, for example, Philip Noel-Baker, *The Arms Race* (1960); Harry Hollins, "A Defensive Weapons System," *Bulletin of the Atomic Scientists* (June, 1982); Mark Sommer, *Beating Our Swords Into Shields* (Miranda, Ca.: Center for Preservative Defense, 1983).

8. Philip Noel-Baker, *The Arms Race*, p. 395.

9. Ibid., p. 400.

10. Jonathan Schell, "The Abolition," *The New Yorker* (January 9, 1984), p. 63.

11. Ibid., pp. 61-62.

12. W.H. Ferry, *A Farewell to Arms* (Nyack, New York: Fellowship Publications, 1978).

13. Freeman Dyson, *Weapons and Hope* (New York: Harper and Row, 1984), p. 258.

14. Ibid., p. 265.

15. Robert Woito, *To End War: A New Approach to International Conflict* (New York: Pilgrim Press, 1982), p. 494.

16. Charles Osgood, *An Alternative to War and Surrender* (Champaign: University of Illinois Press, 1962), p. 9.

17. Ibid., pp. 6, 15, 19.

18. Ibid., p. 34.

19. Amitai Etzioni, "The Kennedy Experiment," in *GRIT I*, Peace Research Reviews, volume 8, number 1 (January, 1979), pp. 62-63.

20. Ibid., p. 64.

21. Franklin Long, "Unilateral Initiatives," *Bulletin of the Atomic Scientists* (May, 1984), pp. 50-54.

22. Thomas Schelling, *The Strategy of Conflict* (Oxford: Oxford University Press, 1960), p. 63.

23. Louis Kriesberg, "Non-Coercive Inducements in International Conflict," *Peace and Change*, VII, 4 (Fall, 1981); reprinted in Burns Weston, *Towards Nuclear Disarmament and Global Security* (Boulder: Westview, 1984), p. 561.

24. Salvador de Madariaga, *Morning Without Noon: Memoirs* (Farnsborough, England: Saxon House, 1974), p. 70.

Nonviolence: Strengths of the Weak

1. Thomas Schelling, quoted in Adam Roberts, *The Strategy of Civilian Defence* (London: Faber, 1967), Note 25.

2. Gene Sharp, *The Politics of Nonviolent Action, Part I (Power and Struggle)* (Boston: Porter Sargent, 1974), p. 8.

3. Gene Sharp, *Social Power and Political Freedom* (Boston: Porter Sargent, 1980), p. 241.

4. George Kennan, *Russia, The Atom, and the West* (New York: Harper and Bros., 1958), pp. 62-65.

5. Sharp, op. cit., pp. 167, 228.

6. "Complementary Forms of Resistance: A Summary of the Report of the Swedish Commission on Resistance," Swedish Official State Reports (SOU, 1984): 10, pp. 4, 19.

7. Gene Keyes, "Force Without Firepower: A Doctrine of Unarmed Military Service," *Co-Evolution Quarterly* (#34) (Summer, 1982), p. 5.

8. Theodor Ebert, "Organizational Preparations for Nonviolent Civilian Defense" (Paper for Oxford Civilian Defense Study Conference, 1964), quoted in Keyes, op. cit., p. 20.

9. Keyes, op. cit., pp. 6-24.

10. Robert Fuller, "A Better Game Than War," *Evolutionary Blues* II (1983).

11. Stephen King-Hall, *Defence in the Nuclear Age* (Nyack, New York: Fellowship Publications, 1959), p. 157.

12. B.H. Liddell Hart, *Deterrence or Defence* (1960), p. 220.

13. Richard Fogg, "Nonmilitary Defense Against Nuclear Threateners and Attackers: A Position Paper" (Stevenson, Maryland: Center for the Study of Conflict, 1983).

14. George Kennan, *The Nuclear Delusion: Soviet-American Relations in the Atomic Age* (New York: Pantheon, 1982), p. 71.

15. Freeman Dyson, *Weapons and Hope* (New York: Harper and Row, 1984), pp. 210-211.

---

**Peace Research:** Beyond "Permanent Pre-Hostilities"

1. Kenneth Boulding, *Stable Peace* (Austin: University of Texas Press, 1978), p. 66.

2. Herbert Kelman, "Reflections on the History and Status of Peace Research," *Conflict Management and Peace Science,* volume 5, number 2 (Spring, 1981), p. 108.

3. Kenneth Boulding, "The Power of Nonconflict," *Journal of Social Issues,* 33, 1 (1977).

4. Kelman, op. cit., p. 107.

5. Richard Falk and Samuel Kim, editors, *The War System: An Interdisciplinary Approach* (Boulder: Westview, 1980).

6. Kenneth Boulding, op. cit., pp. 107-108.

7. Beverly Woodward, "The Abolition of War," *Crosscurrents,* XXXIII, 3 (Fall, 1983), p. 271.

8. Kenneth Boulding, op. cit., p. 101.

9. David Mitrany, *A Working Peace System* (Chicago: Quadrangle, 1966), p. 25.

10. Ibid., p. 35.

11. Ibid., p. 42.

12. Ibid., p. 70.

13. Ibid., p. 98.

**Economic Conversion:** Swords into Services

1. Seymour Melman, editor, *The Defense Economy,* p. 10.
2. Ibid., p. 7.
3. Physicians for Society Responsibility Conference, December 12, 1981, San Francisco, California.

**Negotiation:** Tying is Winning

1. Roger Fisher and William Langer Ury, *Getting to Yes: Negotiating Agreement Without Giving In* (Boston: Houghton Mifflin, 1982), p. 11.
2. Ibid., p. 55.
3. Ibid., p. 11.
4. Ibid., p. 94.

**Game Theory:** Nice Guys Last Longest

1. Ian Hacking, "Winner Take Less," *New York Review of Books* (June 28, 1984), p. 17.
2. Robert Axelrod, *The Evolution of Cooperation* (New York: Basic Books, 1984).
3. Lewis Thomas, "An Argument for Cooperation," *Discover* (August, 1984), p. 68.
4. Ibid., p. 69.
5. Axelrod, op. cit., pp. 173-174.

**Alternative Futurism:** Toward More Practical Utopias

1. Fred Polak, *The Image of the Future* (San Francisco: Jossey-Bass, 1976), p. 19.
2. Ibid., p. 220.
3. Elise Boulding, "The Social Imagination and the Crisis of Human Futures: A North American Perspective," *Forum for Correspondence and Contact,* FCC 13: 2 (February, 1983).

4. Ibid., p. 27.

5. Ibid., pp. 29-33.

6. Ibid., p. 36.

7. Ibid., p. 38.

8. Arthur Waskow, "Looking Forward: 1999," *Our Generation* (Montreal), V: 4 (1968).

9. Joel Kovel, *Against the State of Nuclear Terror* (Boston: South End Press, 1984), pp. 227-228.

10. Margaret Mead, "Towards More Vivid Utopias," in George Kateb, *Utopia* (New York: Atherton Press, 1971), pp. 45-47.

11. Ibid., p. 51.

12. Thomas Kuhn, *The Structure of Scientific Revolutions* (Chicago: University of Chicago Press, 1962), p. 90.

13. Michael Nagler, "Peace as a Paradigm Shift," *Bulletin of the Atomic Scientists* (December, 1981), p. 50.

14. Kuhn, op. cit., p. 77.

15. Walter Lippmann, "The Political Equivalent of War," *Atlantic Monthly* 142 (August, 1928), pp. 181-182.

16. Kuhn, op. cit., pp. 92-93.

17. Polak, op. cit., p. 303.

---

**Conclusion:** Are There Better Games than War?

1. J. Glenn Gray, *The Warriors: Reflections on Men in Battle,* 2nd ed. (New York: Harper and Row, 1970), p. 225.

2. George Kennan, *The Nuclear Delusion,* pp. xxvii, xxix.

3. Robert Fuller, "A Better Game Than War," *Evolutionary Blues* II (1983), pp. 14, 20.

---

**Epilogue:** The Bomb Has Already Fallen

1. Dylan Thomas, "Do Not Go Gentle Into That Good Night," *Poems of Dylan Thomas* (New York: New Directions, 1952).

2. *Voter Options on Nuclear Arms Policy: A Briefing Book for the 1984 Elections* (New York and Providence: The Public Agenda Foundation and Brown University's Center for Foreign Policy Development, 1984), pp. 17-18.

3. Ibid., p. 32.

4. Ibid., p. 43.

5. Ibid., p. 25.

6. Jerome B. Wiesner, "A Militarized Society," *Bulletin of the Atomic Scientists*, 41, 7 (August, 1985), p. 105.

7. Robert Jay Lifton and Richard Falk, *Indefensible Weapons: The Psychological and Political Case Against Nuclearism* (New York: Basic Books, 1982), p. 67.

8. *In the Nuclear Shadow*. A 16 mm. and half-inch VHS videotape, color, 25 minutes. Impact Productions, 1983. Rental: film $20, tape $10.

9. Benina Berger Gould, Susan Moon, Judith van Hoorn, eds., *Growing Up Scared? The Psychological Effect of the Nuclear Threat on Children: Strategies for Action*, Nuclear Ecology Research Project, 1200 Keith Avenue, Berkeley, CA 94708.

10. Lewis Mumford, *The Myth of the Machine: The Pentagon of Power* (New York: Harcourt, Brace, and Jovanovich, 1970). See Chapter 9, "The Nucleation of Power."

11. Paul Brians, "Americans Learn to Love the Bomb," *The New York Times* (July 17, 1985), p. 27. See also Paul Brians, *Nuclear Holocausts: Atomic War in Fiction, 1914-1984* (forthcoming).

12. Robert Jay Lifton, *The Broken Connection* (New York: Touchstone, 1979), p. 376.

13. Alan Wolfe, "Nuclear Fundamentalism Reborn," *World Policy Journal*, II, 1 (Fall, 1984), pp. 91-92.

14. Quoted in Nicholas Humphrey and Robert Jay Lifton, *In a Dark Time* (Cambridge: Harvard University Press, 1984), p. 67.

15. Ibid., pp. 67, 66.

16. Joel Kovel, *Against the State of Nuclear Terror* (Boston: South End Press, 1984), p. 84.

17. Stephen Kull, "Nuclear Arms and the Desire for World Destruction," *Political Psychology*, 4, 3 (1983), p. 579.

18. Alia Johnson, "Why We Should Drop the Bombs," *Evolutionary Blues*, 1, 1, p. 1. Copyright *Co-Evolution Quarterly*.

19. Quoted by Horst-Eberhard Richter, "Living Under the Threat of Nuclear War," in *The Human Cost of Nuclear War*, edited by Stephen Farrow and Alex Chown. (Cardiff: Medical Campaign Against Nuclear Weapons, 1983), p. 99.

20. See Urie Bronfenbrenner, "The Mirror Image in Soviet-American Relations: A Social Psychologist's Report," *Journal of Social Issues*, 17, 3 (1961), pp. 45-50.

21. Jerome Frank, *Sanity and Survival* (New York: Harper and Row, 1966), p. 117.

22. Israel Charny, *How Can We Commit the Unthinkable?* (Boulder: Westview Press, 1982), p. 225.

23. Nicholas Humphrey, "Four Minutes to Midnight." Quoted in Lifton and Humphrey, op. cit., p. 100.

24. John Mack, "Nuclear Winter Is Already Here," *Los Angeles Times* (February 18, 1985), reprinted in *Awakening in the Nuclear Age Journal* (Summer, 1985), p. 31.

25. See Joanna Macy, "Despair Work," *Evolutionary Blues*, I (1981), pp. 36-47. See also Macy, *Despair and Personal Power in the Nuclear Age* (Philadelphia: New Society Publishers, 1983). Interhelp Networking Newsletter, $20/year from P.O. Box 331, Northampton, MA 01061. "Awakening in the Nuclear Age Journal," $20/year from P.O. Box 4742, Berkeley, CA 94704. Fran Peavey, *Heart Politics* (Philadelphia: New Society Publishers, 1985).

# INDEX